A Woman's Angle

Celebrating 20 Years of Women Fly Fishing

Rabbit Jensen

authorHOUSE®

AuthorHouse™
1663 Liberty Drive
Bloomington, IN 47403
www.authorhouse.com
Phone: 1 (800) 839-8640

Published by AuthorHouse   02/23/2016

ISBN: 978-1-5049-8144-6 (sc)
ISBN: 978-1-5049-8143-9 (e)

Library of Congress Control Number: 2016902993

Print information available on the last page.

Any people depicted in stock imagery provided by Thinkstock are models, and such images are being used for illustrative purposes only. Certain stock imagery © Thinkstock.

This book is printed on acid-free paper.

To Mary S. Kuss, founder of the Delaware Valley Women's Fly Fishing Association and its most active member for its entire existence. Editing the newsletter for its first ten years, creating the club's structure and mission, hosting events, always ready to pitch in for any club activity; and above all, teaching, guiding, and sharing her passion for fly-fishing with hundreds of people over the years. May she continue to be the heart and soul of the club for another twenty years.

Foreword

Immersed in Fly Fishing and Writing, Just for the Fun Of It!

I've been wrapped up in the world of fly fishing for over thirty-five years and have owned and operated my fly fishing guide service, *Women's Flyfishing®* for twenty-nine of them. I started my business to help introduce more women to a sport that most of them knew nothing about, and, since I live in Alaska, I also endeavored to bring them into the incredible outdoor environment where I live. After a bit I learned about several fly fishing clubs for women that were in existence, and collaborated with some of them to help grow our sport.

As time went by, my web site www.womensflyfishing.net generated more and more interest, as did my electronic newsletter. Established women's clubs like the ones in Albuquerque, San Francisco, and Seattle helped new clubs develop in various areas all around the country, and even in other countries. Not all of the original fly fishing clubs for women are still in operation, but many still exist. One of the best is in operation in Pennsylvania.

The Delaware Valley Women's Fly Fishing Association has been offering women the opportunity to enter the wonderful world of fly fishing for two decades! They took up the challenge of creating a women's club when there were just a few others around, especially on the east coast, and they have maintained it for the benefit of dozens and dozens of women taking up fly fishing in their area.

Over all these years they've faithfully gotten together for at least two fishing excursions in each of the fishable months for everything from bluegill to bluefish. The trips range from day trips to local streams to fully guided overnight adventures. In the off-season you'll find them offering introductory fly fishing classes and fly tying clinics to help other women get started, holding monthly meetings with well-known professional speakers, and doing other types of networking, mentoring, and socializing.

Over all these years they've also maintained one of the very best quarterly newsletters of any fly fishing club I know. A small group of members make sure that "A Women's Angle" comes out regularly, and it always contains excellent articles on various aspects of fly fishing. Now, in acknowledgement of their twentieth anniversary, and the never ending dedication of the wonderful newsletter editor, Rabbit Jensen, they've put over fifty of these newsletter articles into a book of very enjoyable women's writing.

I was one of the speakers for a club meeting during a trip east to introduce my fourth book, *"Pacific Salmon Flies: New Ties and Old Standbys"* at the International Fly Tying Symposium in 2012, and was lucky enough to be able to stay for a visit and some fishing with members of the club. We wined and dined at one member's comfortable house, we wadered-up to chase brownies in a small, golden leafed creek, we had a presentation at a club meeting, and I also got introduced to the Hawk Mountain Sanctuary, world-famous raptor-watching spot. Since then I've written my fifth book, *"Rookie No More: The Fly Fishing Novice Gets Guidance From a Pro"* and all that culminated in my being asked to write the Foreword to this delightful new anthology that the club is creating entitled *"A Woman's Angle: Celebrating 20 Years of Women Fly Fishing."* I got a sneak-peek into some of the various articles in their draft form, and was very, very impressed. This is definitely not just a book for members of the club. I'm betting that fly anglers everywhere will embrace it with gusto.

I love seeing women writing about their experiences, their challenges, and even their not-so-great days with humor and delight. Beware that some of the articles might bring a tear to your eye, but they'll all bring a smile to your face and a chuckle to your voice. You're going to fall in love with all these authors and hope that you will see more of their work in fly fishing magazines in days to come. There's lots and lots of talent out there, and when you are reading this book, I'm betting that you'll be reading work from some of our sport's up-and-coming authors.

Best Fishes, Cecilia "Pudge" Kleinkauf

Author:
-*Rookie No More: The Fly Fishing Novice Gets Guidance from a Pro (Epicenter Press, 2016)*
-*Pacific Salmon Flies: New Ties & Old Standbys (Frank Amato Publications, 2012)*
- *Fly Fishing for Alaska's Arctic Grayling: Sailfish of the North (Frank Amato Publications, 2009)*

Benjamin Franklin Award-winning Books
-*River Girls: Fly Fishing for Young Women, (Johnson Books, 2006)*
-*Fly Fishing Women Explore Alaska, (Epicenter Press, 2003)*

Preface

The editor of an anthology only does a fraction of the work involved in its production. This book, spanning the first twenty years of the Delaware Valley Women's Fly Fishing Association, owes as much to the people who started the club and kept it going as to the many talented writers who submitted articles to the newsletter during those years.

I'd like to single out four people for special recognition: former newsletter editors Mary S. Kuss and Joan Hackmann-Gaul, club historian and archivist Lisa Miller, and our ever-patient proof-reader, Mary Gibney. Whether providing copies of the earliest newsletters or contact information for members that have been out of touch for a decade, rating articles, reminding me of great writers I'd forgotten, or inspiring me to keep going on this massive project, these women have been a constant source of support.

Over the years dozens of dedicated people have worked to keep the club going and growing: Board members, event hosts, instructors, and those who worked behind-the-scenes keeping us all fishing. They deserve all the praise I can heap on them. I'd also like to recognize our business sponsors that donated goods, time, guest speakers or fly-tiers, and promoted the club in their shops or online.

Many writers have contributed fine articles to the newsletter from its first issue to the present, and I'd like to thank all these ladies—and the single gentleman whose work appears in this book; when you read his piece you'll understand why—for giving us their best.

Most of all, I'd like to thank the hundreds of women who were DVWFFA members over its first two decades. Without them, there would be no club and no book. Many of them have fished with me and enriched the outing; many of them have become dear friends. Lastly, I must mention the former members and friends of the club that are now casting their flies on some Heavenly stream. They are remembered, and missed, every time one of us old-timers wets a line.

Rabbit Jensen

Contents

Introduction

The Origins of the DVWFFA
By Mary S. Kuss

I started fishing when I was six years old, and started fly fishing when I was fifteen. The details of how those events came about are a story for another day, but suffice to say that I always managed to find a way to go fishing. Virtually all of that fishing was done in the company of men—relatives, co-workers, friends and acquaintances. None of my childhood girlfriends were interested in fishing, and they thought I was more than a little weird for liking it so much.

In 1970, soon after beginning college at Widener University (then PMC Colleges) in Chester, PA, I met and became friends with Rabbit Jensen. Much to my delight she became interested in the sport. In a rather atypical progression, she first tied flies and later took up fly fishing. But most importantly, I now had a woman fishing buddy.

She was the only one, however, for many years. Fishing with her, and with my male fishing friends, was wonderful. But I couldn't help thinking on occasion how nice it would be to have more women fishing friends. Still, life seemed good and I didn't have much motivation to do anything more than enjoy what I had.

Then, in the spring of 1995, my comfortable situation began to unravel a bit at the edges. In the apparent throes of a mid-life crisis, my previously quite tolerant husband suddenly had a problem with my annual spring fishing trip to Potter County with some of my best fishing buds, all guys. Their wives and girlfriends even offered to go to bat for me with Bob, to assure him that they were fine with the trip as they had been for the past six years. Everyone was there to catch trout, and all concerned parties knew it. But Bob would not be swayed. He kept saying, "It just doesn't look good for my wife to spend a week in a cabin with four guys." After much discussion I finally decided that as irrational as this attitude was, and as much as it grieved me to do so, if he felt that strongly about it I would have to give up the trip.

Now there was a problem to solve. Once again I had to find a way to do my fishing. If I couldn't go on fishing trips with the boys anymore, I had darned well better find some women to go fishing with. This was the impetus needed to get me moving on the attempt to start up a women's fly fishing club. I pursued a number of contacts, through fly shops and Trout Unlimited chapters in the area.

After a lot of telephone time, I finally felt that I had enough interested women to get things under way. The organizational meeting for the new women's fly fishing club was held on January 9, 1996 at the Townhouse Restaurant in Media, Pennsylvania. Nine women were in attendance: Dawn Stevens, Fran Witman, Eileen Gallagher (now Eileen Baltz), Judith Palmer, Eleanor Peterson, Stephanie Arndt, Alexis Hillman, Mary Clarke, and myself. It's interesting to note that all but two of those original nine are still active with the club.

I drafted up some proposed by-laws to bring to the meeting, based on the standard Trout Unlimited by-laws. I also chose a preliminary name for the club: the Philadelphia Women Flyfishers. Dawn agreed to serve as the first president, but with a condition. As a resident of Wilmington, Delaware, she did not like the idea of the reference to Philadelphia in the club name. She proposed Delaware Valley Women's Fly Fishing Association. Although this seemed a bit unwieldy to some of us, all present were willing to defer to her on this point. After all, anyone willing to serve as the first president of the club was certainly entitled to some say in the matter.

Although I was quite unaware of it, and the timing was purely coincidental, I could not have picked a more propitious time to start up a women's fly fishing club. We were on the threshold of a major upswing in women's involvement in all outdoor sports. The *Becoming an Outdoors Woman* program would soon begin, sponsored by state fish and game agencies throughout the country and designed to introduce women to a whole list of outdoor activities. Women's fishing clubs began springing up like mushrooms all over the map. The time was definitely right.

Dawn was DVWFFA president for the next six years, serving with tremendous dedication and hard work. The Board of Directors repeatedly waived the term limit specified in the club by-laws, since Dawn was willing to continue to serve and everyone was glad for her to do it. I don't think anyone realized how much work she was doing for our organization until, for personal reasons, she declined another term.

Dawn's departure left a yawning chasm that was nearly the undoing of the club. After six months without a Board meeting, it seemed like the DVWFFA would simply fade away if something wasn't done to jump start us again. I knew that the club had become important to a number of the members, including myself, and I didn't want to just let it die without a fight. So I called a meeting at my house of four people I felt would be willing to do what was necessary to resuscitate the DVWFFA. Everyone pitched in, and their initiative and effort started the club on the road to its current solid status.

As we approach our 20th anniversary year, all of our members both past and present can be justifiably proud of our organization. We've made a difference in the lives of a great many women fly fishers, and hopefully will continue to do so for the next twenty years and beyond.

*For more information on the Delaware Valley Women's
Fly Fishing Association, visit our website at:*
www.dvwffa.org

Donna Trexler fishing for salmon on the Miramichi.

Riverquest
By Lynette Monteiro Musten

"I've found the perfect river for you." My fly fishing friend's practiced voice carried all the promise of flashing rainbows. It was hard to separate his professional tone selling hope and salvation from his fishing tone selling big fish on long, tight lines. Well, what the heck, I thought, it was time for a vacation anyway. And, why not a fishing vacation? Certainly my family was open to the suggestion. Mum on vacation? Away from the books and the phones and the computer? No nagging about laundry or dirty dishes or hopelessly clinging dog hairs on the rugs and sofas? If my growing, passionate affair with fly fishing took them places they've been begging to go, then they were the last to resist.

Perhaps that was the method in my husband's madness when the fly rod and reel appeared under the Christmas tree three years ago. I remember (they remember more fondly) putting the reel on the rod and trying to figure out how to hold it. "It's upside down, dear," the Big Fuzzy Guy corrected from behind the safety of the frying pan. That was it for a year. I'm not given to not knowing everything all at once. A trait that is either a quality or a delight depending on the stamina of my company, I'm told.

I'm also not given to giving up. The milestones that mark the way from the Bearbrook that flows past my home to the Crowsnest in Alberta 2,000 miles away are not difficult to find. Rods, reels, and indescribable (in numbers and features) flies, books, magazines, videos and endless correspondences—all brilliant sensory data. I get out in the real waters, too: flailing at trees that snatched my flies from perfect backcasts; puzzling at rocks that moved like bass and bass that sulked like rocks; contorting with canoe paddles and fly rods with screaming reels.

Somewhere, sometime in the myriad of failure experiences and a rollercoastering learning curve, a quiet rebellion begins. It starts on an evening standing in the middle of my brook. Facing downstream, I watch the riffles and the blossoming circles of stream chub and bass feeding in the deeper pools. My friends ask if I live in the country because I treasure the silence. I have no way of explaining that I live here because I treasure the sounds. The flash and thrash of the chub attacking the fly is bracketed by the hysterical flapping of a duck startled from its cover and the sensuously paced drumming of the blue heron patrolling the skylength of the stream. These fuse abruptly into another sound: "Mom! Dad says dinner's in half an hour." The rebellion begins when I realize I really have an hour if I claim I'm just being fashionably late for dinner.

My family watches horrified and bemused as I learn to hike, canoe, scramble rocks, slide down undercut river banks. The ability to tolerate wilderness expands beyond the rose garden and back fields into local lakes and rivers. By spring I'm ready for the text-book fishing trip. I bill the Crowsnest to my family as an 'explore' in the best Winnie-the-Pooh tradition. They don't buy it.

The Big Fuzzy and the A-1 Kid huddle together making their own plans knowing (better than I) that they will be abandoned to their own devices on some river bed. Knowing my courage is greater than my knowledge, I book a guide to coach me through the waters. He's a Special-Ed teacher in his other life, he smiles. I know he sees through the compliance to the problem child in full bloom; I also know there's no principal's office open within 100 kilometers of Burmis Lake. By the end of the day, I also learn more corrective measures than I thought possible. We hike what seems a million miles and cast as many times for each mile. I try to distract him: Does he think women cast better than men? Does he think women are more likely to admit to their limits than men? His replies are strongly behavioral and gender issues melt in the face of pragmatics. *You have a good strong backcast*, he says, *but you collapse on the frontcast. Put the fly in that slick but make sure you get in that upstream mend. Try for an exactly forty-five degree angle when you're casting across. We're going to have to scramble that last turn; do you want me to take your rod or can you manage?*

The next day I fish the same stretch of water where it doglegs around a gravel bank. Fast and deeply colored, frontcast running with the wind, I hold little hope of finding the rainbows. At this point to cast well is less important than to cast well enough. The wind buffets me flinging the backcast into a heap. I look around in frustration: alone with the sounds of water, wind, and foliage. For a moment I want to be back in time when

I was a too-busy wife, mother, and self; demanded of and demanding. Although I understand that better than collapsing frontcasts, being blown about in the course of getting something done is also familiar. I wait for the between-gust quiet and toss in a cast. Not pretty but effective. The flash and thrash of the rainbow welds past and present knowledge. I bring it to net and snap the picture. It sits on my desk, brilliant sensory data haloed with light sparkles off the perfect river.

Summer 1996

Cynthia Sarnoski catches a spring smallmouth bass.

Life's Lessons Learned on Penn's Creek
By Erin Mooney

Wading Penn's Creek, the famed central Pennsylvania trout stream, I was forced to come to terms with my own limitations and the restrictions imposed on me by nature. I learned a lot about myself during the two days that I fished there; about limits, humility, and other life lessons.

It was late June, just after the prolific Green Drake hatch. The stream was a virtual spin cycle of insect activity with sporadic hatches, insects of all kinds bursting forth into flight all along the stream. Trout were rising, becoming airborne for seconds at a time. The full warmth of the summer was not yet settled on that part of the country, but a sticky, thick humidity was beginning to envelop the days in its embrace. Wild pansies were giving forth to tiger lilies and the light green landscape was evolving to a darker, more lush quilt of verdant shades.

The section of Penn's Creek where I fished was not as clear as many other streams I had explored. Large, mossy submerged rocks became definite barriers to my wading speed. Nevertheless, I plunged ahead. Though my fishing companions gingerly fished their way alongside the bank, staying close to land, I had my sights set on a fallen tree on the other side of the stream. The current was strong as I made my way across. As my feet slipped on hidden rocks, I felt like I was wearing banana peels on my feet, not sturdy felt-soled waders. I envisioned myself falling in the water, my rod tossed downstream in a wash of white water. My heart began to pound, adrenaline began to shoot into my system. I looked upstream, only to see one of my companions sliding on an unseen underwater boulder. My own confidence began to wane.

"Stop your worrying," I told myself. "You are young, you're a good swimmer, and for god sakes, you are a Pisces, a fish in water!" I felt rather silly for being afraid. Even though dusk was falling, my determination to cross the stream was renewed. After numerous fly line snags in the fallen tree, I was forced to walk over to retrieve my fly from the tip of a branch, located in a whirlpool of water. Again, the adrenaline began to seep into my veins as I swung around the log and caught myself on one of its arms, dislodging the fly and muttering a few choice words aloud. Through some tricky maneuvering and lucky balancing, I made my way out of that eddy, back to the other side of the stream.

Comparing notes with my companions, they were all surprised at the level of wading difficulty that we were presented with on Penn's. One woman, a wise person who was always well-equipped and well-dressed as well, had bought a wading staff after hearing about the degree of wading difficulty on the stream. "Wading staff? Who needs a wading staff?" I thought to myself. I wrote it off as something *I* would never use.

On the next morning, I was ready to take to the stream to tempt a few of the fish I'd seen rising the evening before. With the help of a local guide, we headed to a spot where fish were clearly feeding. Within several casts, my Griffith's Gnat had tempted three trout to take my fly. Though the water was warm, the native browns were not sluggish, but hungry and active.

My fishing partner moved upstream a dozen or so feet, behind an outcropping of shrubs. I wished her well, took a step aside and brought in my fly line to change my fly. Within seconds, I had lost my footing and was floundering in the water. Water rushed inside my belted chest waders and my feet scrambled to send my body upright. I began to hyperventilate and seriously thought I might wash downstream. Trying desperately to maintain hold of my rod, I sought a foothold among the rocks that had sent me reeling.

After several tries, I was able to regain my stance. I turned to get the attention of my fishing companion, but she was nowhere to be seen. My heart pounding, hot tears welling in my eyes, I made my way out of the water to sit on the bank. It all happened so fast. Unbelievable. I played it back in slow motion and I couldn't comprehend how little it took to move me from a casual position to being immersed in water.

As I thanked whatever deity I turn to in times like this, I unzipped my vest to get out of my waders and I saw my lower vest pocket open and empty. I had lost my flies. Dozens of Elk Hair Caddis, brand new red foam ladybugs, a handful of Blue-Winged Olives, a misshapen black Wooly Bugger (the first fly I had ever tied), and over 150 other flies had washed downstream within seconds. That box had held my entire year of fly fishing in its grasp. In my other pocket sat my soggy, brand new zoom lens camera. Perfectly sized for a fishing vest, it had been intended to document the many fish I was sure to catch that day. Needless to say, it would never capture such a hot moment on film. It was indeed an expensive fall I took.

In retrospect, after the tears had dried and the sadness at my financial losses had dissolved into my ever-expanding catalog of life experiences, I realized I had learned a lot. Although I had read quite a bit about stream maneuvering and precautionary measures, I had always viewed myself as pretty much invincible. That experience taught me I am not.

I didn't fish the rest of that day. Instead, I looked in vain for my flies and contemplated my cavalier attitude. That night, I was presented with a new fly box filled with flies gathered from the vests of friends. Though I still remember the dozens of flies collected during my first year of fishing, I have been able to let go and just be thankful that was all I lost. Now, when I tie on a Royal Wulff or a beetle that was donated to my new collection, I think of the generosity of the women I fished with that weekend on Penn's Creek.

I still have not bought a wading staff, but it is on my list of future purchases. My fly box is now labeled with my name and address and I'm in the process of devising a way to attach it to my vest.

As for Penn's Creek, I will always remember this trip there as a sobering time in my fly fishing career, where I learned to respect nature and give myself to her power when necessary.

Autumn 1997

Why Did I Take Up Fly Fishing?
By Susan Eggert

As a result of my expert and delicate presentation, the cricket fly landed squarely between my shoulder blades. This was the product of what I call my "Flail Cast." Now the real test of my fly fishing skill was about to begin. How do I remove this wad of black moose hair (and more importantly, the hook it is attached to) while standing in a very rickety, very unstable canoe? I could have removed my button-fronted shirt but, I was afraid that adding sleeves to the tangle of fly line, long blonde braid, rod and canoe paddle would have just been too much for me to navigate. My frustration level had already passed the point where I ask myself, "*Why* did I take up fly fishing?" One more complication would have been too much; would have literally sent me over the edge.

Reaching my left hand up and around behind me while I held the rod in my right and commanded the rest of my body to keep the dang canoe steady, I released the cricket from its denim snag. This is one form of "catch and release."

That scene was mercifully executed with only one discreet witness, my dog Lorna. Once I recovered my dignity I began to cast again. This time I slowed down and watched the line, analyzing the effects of my timing and rhythm. As each cast gained in grace a sense of calm took the place of frustration. I began to maneuver the canoe around the pond's edge, willing my casts to land in the vicinity of that spot near the reeds where a big feeding bass had just mimicked a small hand grenade exploding inches beneath the surface. Once or twice the cast did land there and I managed to bring in a three pound bass and a feisty bluegill.

In that brief hour before sunset I rediscovered a few of the many reasons to fly fish. In descending order of preference they are: to catch fish, to meet the challenge of the cast and improve with every effort, and to learn how to dislodge flies from your person with as much finesse as possible.

Gliding the canoe toward shore across the darkening surface of the pond another larger reason became evident. With every silent purple and silver ring appearing like surprise gifts on the water, one more worry disappeared. *What* phone bill, taxes, wobbly career, relationship to revive? In that moment I only needed to wonder if that was the call of a hawk from the top of the sassafras tree. The fourth reason? Knowing that those rings, that hawk, and the sight of the astonishing orange flame of the alchemized sky would all meld together to fortify me for tomorrow.

Winter 1997

Kettle Creek in June
By Mary S. Kuss

Cold gray ledges of slate
blanketed with moss,
draped in ferns,
and overhung by hemlock.

Crystal water cold and clear,
singing an endless chuckling song
as it runs along
its eternal course.

The wild trout, wary and quick,
clean and brightly speckled,
rises to my fly
if all is right.

Leaping, flashing, thrashing,
until I can ease the hook free.
A pause, a wiggle, he darts away
as quickly as he came.

Verdant meadows lie opposite the steep ledges,
meadows full of hoppers,
herringbone on their legs,
tobacco juice on their lips.

Sweetly scented air,
a cooling breeze,
Slate Drakes on the wing,
blackflies a-buzz.

The music of the stream
is accompanied by bird song:
the Yellowthroat and the Oriole,
the Yellow Warbler and the Rose-Breasted Grosbeak.

A raven gives a discordant croak,
a sound of wild country.
Here the hand of man
still touches lightly.

Written along Kettle Creek, June 13, 1996

Erin Dietrich fishing Kettle Creek in June.

Variations on a Theme
By Lynette Monteiro Musten

"Yes, hello, we'd like to know more about your Compliance Training program." The voice on the phone is efficient, business-like. I take a quick scan around my study. The call has come to the house, not the office. I've picked up the phone in the study, one hand on the receiver, one holding down a rebellious hackle on a dry fly. *Compliance?* I want to say, *Lady, I can barely get a dead feather to listen to me!* But she's in no mood for insight training.

"I can't get him to do anything. Every time I ask he ends up forcing me to yell!"

I still don't know if she's referring to a child or a dog. It really doesn't matter and I have been taken to task several times for saying the training's all the same. Wedging the phone into my shoulder, I return to the fly in the vise and settle in for a long listen.

"He's four and no one agrees on how to do this."

"To do…?"

"Dress."

"Ah. Dressing is important."

I take the fly out of the vise and choose another hook. Crimping down the barb and setting it firmly in the vise, I reach for the nearest thread and stop. *Dressing begins with the foundations,* I mutter into the phone. *What am I trying to do here,* I continue murmuring. *Ah, right… first build the right base. So we start with the right color because that's where we want to end up.*

"I'm not sure I understand," she says.

"Oh. Um, er… you have to have a goal."

All right. Wrap the thread tightly starting at the eye and working back to the bend. *Slow and steady,* I mutter, *you can't rush this stage. It just makes everything else hard to keep on.*

"I understand," she says.

A quick flash of cement over the thread wrap seals it and ensures durability. *Thanks, Mary,* I nod, causing the phone to slide off my shoulder.

"Who's Mary?" The voice comes from under the desk.

I wedge the phone back in place. "Mary?"

"Yes. Mary. You said: Thanks, Mary."

"Oh… another trainer," I congratulate myself on thinking quickly. "She's good on the details."

"Ah. She trained you."

"Yeah… that's it! Yup." Well, it's not exactly a lie.

OK, you've started with the base. Now think: where am I going to be in two months? Visions of long, lazy stretches of river flash through my mind as I take a deep breath. I can almost smell the pines and feel the rounded pebbles and crunching slate underfoot.

"Disneyland."

"Pardon?"

"Disneyland. We promised him Disneyland if he can get himself dressed in the mornings."

There's no fish in Disneyland, I start to say. Well, not unless you count that syrupy mermaid. Instead I say, "Rewards are good."

"We thought it was a bribe."

"Bribes are good, too," I shrug, almost sending the phone into another underworld foray. Tie two flies a night and you get dessert. Works for me. Get the proportions right on that Hornberg and you get ice cream too. Good thing I hate ice cream. More than that, I'd have to promise myself that new BMW Roadster if I ever got a fly tied that was smaller than a #14. My ego has taken a beating lately on the dries and itty-bitty eye-crossing sizes.

"We were worried that the bribe… er… reward was not in proportion."

"Proportions are very important. You just don't get the right drift…"

"I beg your pardon?" She's incensed. "I'm really trying to learn all I can here!"

"No, no," I scramble to refocus. "You just don't want to get a *rift*… a rift in your family over rewards and bribes. It's not important."

"Ah."

Stay focused, I chastise myself under my breath.

"Yes!" she exclaims. "That's exactly his problem! He can't stay focused! And we get disorganized! So what you are saying is *we* should stay focused on our goal and work with a good foundation!"

"Er… right… that's it… exactly!" I'm wrestling the green chenille into a loopy tail. *Don't force it.*

"No, no… we won't. What next?" Her voice is awe-filled.

Securing the loop, I let the bobbin hang and start on the body wraps. *Wait, take it back to the top*—I'm referring to the thread that's still hanging on the bend.

"You mean the foundations? I thought we were done with that?"

"No, no," I mutter. "Plan one step ahead, work one step behind."

"That's wonderful! Thank you! So we shouldn't rush him but we should be prepared ourselves for the next thing we want."

Right. The bobbin swings happily behind the eye and I wrap the chenille to the front. *Close the gap; you know how important that is.*

"Yes, we often forget that we were children too." Her voice drifts off into her own memories.

A few quick turns of the thread and the head seals the miniscule opening in the eye. *Cut thread and finish off with a cementing.*

"Oh, I'm not sure I'm ready to cut the thread with him. He's only four, you know." She sounds dubious now about the whole conversation. "I think you're just rushing *me*, now. But thank you for all your advice. I know dressing him doesn't seem like such a big thing, but… well… we'd hate for him to turn out like… well… you know… a… a weenie. I don't think our egos could handle it." She laughs, embarrassed.

I lean back to admire my handiwork. Sometimes turning out a Weenie is not such a bad thing for one's ego.

Spring 1998

If Rivers Remember
By Susan Eggert

Tonight the December wind must be lifting little whitecaps off the surface of the Susquehanna River just three miles from where I sit huddled next to my wood stove. Here the river is nearly half a mile broad as it blends into the saltwater of the Chesapeake Bay. In among the giant boulders the river holds such fish as the feisty smallmouth, big ol' catfish, and now fewer striped bass than just a week or so ago as they are moving into the deeper waters of the Bay itself.

As winter sidles in for good, those of us who fish are moving into different waters, too; mainly the ones coursing through either our imaginations or, if we are lucky, our memories. If rivers remember, perhaps I could walk to the edge of the brackish water near home and ask the river to help me recall the gleaming native brook and brown trout I caught months ago and hundreds of miles north in the tiny tributaries of the West Branch of the Susquehanna. How long would it take a trout-shaped piece of water to tumble down out of the quiet forests where bear and grouse live, into broader streams which join the main branch and flow south through Harrisburg, under the rumbling racket of highway bridges, into Maryland to pass the big rock where I often go to watch bald eagles cruising the expansive water for a dinner of white perch?

If the river and I timed it just right that same sliver of water which once held a ten-inch brown trout might meet me at the rock and act as the mnemonic I need to remember the warm autumn day in Potter County when I caught and released that trout into the clear water of Young Woman's Creek. I'll do my best while sitting at my computer three miles up the hill from the river's flow.

I had been to Potter County the year before, and for the last hour of this year's long five hour drive I planned the logistics of getting myself to a certain bend on Kettle Creek with just enough time for half a dozen casts prior to sunset. When I arrived at the cabin I found a note explaining that the others were fishing on one of the many streams within just a few miles' drive of the cabin. I wouldn't have time to find them on that stream so I implemented my Kettle Creek plan and was standing at the bend just as the ridge to the west cast a shadow across the water.

I immediately broke a personal record with the first cast onto the riffles below a pool. I caught the smallest fall fish or creek chub that I had ever seen! Well, the best laid plans. There were other elements at work against my plan on that evening. In my mind's eye I was remembering the Kettle Creek from the previous year and, like people, rivers sometimes change dramatically in twelve months. The water level was very low and some of the pools I remembered were no longer pools at all. The previous year I caught many stocked rainbows in a run formed by a blown-down tree. This year the log was gone and the whole character of that spot on the creek was altered. With dark descending I walked back along the creek toward my car chastising myself for expecting the creek to have gone unchanged in the past year.

Friday evening was spent reminiscing about last year's trip with some of the repeat customers. The disappointment of learning that Lynette Musten and Betsy Miraglia would be leaving in the morning was assuaged just a bit by Lynette's gift of a just-tied Caddis fly. That fly is kept just above the bill of my fishing hat to remind me that the human-to-human connections made while fishing are at least as important as the human-to-fish connections.

And if one of the connections you've made is with Mary Kuss and you both happen to be in Potter County, Pennsylvania you are sure to be introduced to some of the most beautiful trout water anywhere. On Saturday morning we drove south out of the little village of Oleona and into the Sproul State Forest. That day we would fish Young Woman's Creek. Mary and I decided we would fish together moving upstream until we met up with others in the group. In some notes I made about the trip as I was driving home I scribbled the words "siren-like pools." Those words were meant to help me remember the inebriating effect that lovely stream had on me.

Despite our plan to fish upstream I was compelled to walk downstream after just one fleeting look into the distance. The creek was small with long runs of riffles shimmering in the fall light. When I gazed downstream I saw pools shining out from hallways of overhanging trees lit and dazzling in bright foliage. The mossy banks would give way to slate ledges that disappeared into the water. Beyond one gorgeous pool would be another. One might be formed by a downed tree sure to harbor at least one shy native trout. So I found myself walking quietly, trance-like, along the bank, thoroughly intoxicated by what was surrounding me. So mesmerized was I that I had forgotten to fish! At some point I shook myself loose from the trance and began to walk upstream. It wasn't until Mary came back looking for me and told me she had already caught six fish that I began to concentrate on the task at hand. With Mary's help I cast to a little brookie hanging in an eddy and caught it. Then, seconds after Mary was out of sight, I caught my fish to remember at a spot where a smaller stream met Young Woman's. With some contortions I managed to keep the trout safely in the water while one-handedly retrieving my camera from my vest and snapping a picture. The bright spawning colors were captured adequately on film: the powdery blue rings around the dark spots and the bright red speckles. It is no wonder writers refer to these fish as jewels.

More jewels and gems in the form of fish were caught as I moved in the direction of our planned meeting place. All five of us had caught fish on Young Woman's Creek. And though no one mentioned it, I suspect that I was not alone in falling under the spell of that irresistibly beautiful place.

We finished the day back on the Kettle Creek because we wanted to introduce the catch-and-release section to two women who had never fished it. It is in that section where one might catch some larger stocked fish. As Mary and I walked along the bank we peered into the water and spotted a **large** trout at the head of some riffles. Mary told me to walk below it and then cast up to it. I said something like, "That fish is so darned big it scares me!" With just a few casts I managed to introduce myself to Ms. Large Fish via my four-weight rod and a tan Elk Hair Caddis. Quite some fun! Downstream Mary was hosting a rowdy party and introducing herself to lots of fish until it became too dark for her to see the hors d'oeuvres she was serving, and we headed back to the cabin.

That evening some of the more conscientious anglers pulled out well-worn journals and began to make notes about the weekend's fishing. They might list in great detail the weather conditions, flies used, wildlife spotted, numbers of fish caught. While the journals are wonderful tools for improving future fishing efforts, I would imagine too that they get opened during the coldest months of the year so that the joy of those hours spent on the sparkling water can be released again and again into the long winter evenings.

My notes? "Maple, oak, hickory, beech. Russet ferns, spawning male trout in stream not a foot wide, siren-like pools, dreams." What was "dreams" about? I think I had dreamt of the trout at the far reaches of the Susquehanna watershed before I had traveled north to find them there. I had hoped that if the dreams became reality they might find their way back to me again in memories as I waited out the months of winter in a place where all of those quick streams have long been transformed into a giant river, the largest to meet the Bay.

And those memories have found me here on the frigid first day of December. Thinking of the Susquehanna River just down the hillside did help, along with the gift fly, a few photos, an old Pennsylvania map, and the persistent magic of the Potter County trout streams.

Winter 1998

Reflections in a Transparent Stream
By Lynette Monteiro Musten

"Nothing under heaven is softer or weaker than water, and yet nothing is better for attacking what is hard and strong, because of its immutability." —Tao te ching #78

The waters of the river that runs by my window thicken; toughening against the winter wind that blows, northeast, chilling, sweeping summer before it. I had no chance to fish the river this year. With the opportunity to deepen a sense of self that is grounded in independence, fishing overly familiar riffly runs with a few pools of bass and chub seemed a negligible challenge.

June: The Credit River is bounded by thick forest growth where we're fishing this June afternoon. My thoughts are fragmented and light sears from the surface of the water. The rod feels strangely weightless in my hand and I'm frustrated to find the reels of tippet material are back at the truck. The guide points out the differences in the shades of green growth seen through the flow around our ankles. Oxygen content, temperature, shadow and light. The words soothe as information always does for me and I feel rooted in the stones, caressed into stillness by the water. Over the afternoon, we move no more than 50 or 60 feet fishing with a deliberate care and concentration: form, rhythm, pause, form, rhythm, pause. A hawk skims the treetops and he says, "That was you." I look up confused, thinking he means something metaphysical, then realize I'd missed a take. He smiles and notes that a confluence of mindfulness of both waterline and treeline comes with time.

July, journal entry: First solo canoe trip of the season. The lake is grey and windswept forcing me to paddle head down with heavy muscled strokes, tacking across to the farther shore. The curves of the land break the headwind intermittently giving moments to catch my breath until I tie off at the first campsite.

After setting up, it takes about three hours just to stop moving. I keep wanting to *do* something. The books I brought are interesting but too intense. For awhile the sun is too bright, the wind too loud, the water too cold. The canoe is tied off but the waves slam it against the shoreline making a racket. I keep trying to tell myself it will be fine but finally pull it up the slope to ground. Then silence: the wind dies, the trees stop singing, the water stills. I feel like I'd pulled *everything* to shore.

I canoe the perimeter of the north end of the lake for two hours. There are marshes and inlets I'd never known about. The water is black glass and the cedar strip cuts through it without a sound. Never in my life had I thought I was capable of this: of being alone, of feeling safe with myself, of being quiet. At the last turn I let it drift into the reeds and watch the beavers building a dam. A loon swims by with her two still-fuzzy babies and I follow them for awhile then return to the campsite. Curled up on the rock, I am dozing when some canoeists swing by and one fellow asks if I own the rock. I laugh and say, *No, we're negotiating a partnership.* His wife offers me a peanut butter sandwich; I guess I look a bit in need of nurturance.

August: The wings of the plane cut eastwards through the dense clouds, water in another form filling the sky. Days before in yet another different state, it had spun around my waders vibrating signals though the river. The Livingstone, the Crowsnest, the Rocking Horse and an unnamed stream that will be the source of many years of photography. There the glacial colors absorbed and reflected back a muted light and the snow-tipped mountains dominated the horizon, censoring any feelings of superiority I generated with strike, set and netting of cutthroats and rainbows. Standing under the scrutiny of such solidity, emotions surface as the line straightens in front of me: It's a quiet hope to connect with the deepest, darkest part of the river and be ready for whatever it offers. When I bow to release the shimmering trout, I see my reflection in the opaque water, backed by grey stone. In that moment I realize the contract I have entered with the circle of nature and life: to acknowledge that the connection I am granted is real and to respond with honor.

October: Looking down from a ridge into the waters of Kettle Creek, I sense more than see the late afternoon light cast long upstream. In the transparent water the trout line up as if following the direction of quantized energy. It's an overpowering sight, this absolute reality of what I've been trying to reach and touch all day. They're large and move languidly or create stillness in the current, effortless in their own connections. Coming across the ledges above them, it becomes a futile task to cast the line without the light and the stream's clarity betraying my position. In time, I understand the irony of how the clarity of water protects both fish and, sometimes fisher. Wanting is perhaps a more powerful teacher than having. Mostly, I marvel at their determination: They hold in agitated patterns but don't retreat. I think they know in some ineffable way that I'm the one who has to move on, that part of my contract is to try but not to torment. As I continue back up to the ridge, I realize that simply seeing through the water into their lives has been enough.

December: The steam from the coffee swirls over the edge of the mug as I stand on the balcony and watch the river slowly carve around sheets of new ice. Resolutions of committing more time to the things that form and shape my life drift through. Time on this river, time on this land, knowing I am part, and not just an observer, of the changes in wood and water. And, finally there is an understanding that the foundation of these promises is an unshakable faith that takes my vision past the sight-blocking ice and into the deepest pools that now protect the bass for next year.

Winter 1997

Infinite Gravida
By Beth Wilson

When a woman becomes pregnant, her doctor refers to her pregnancy as "gravida." If she is pregnant for the first time, she is a "prima gravida," and every pregnancy thereafter is numbered to keep track of how many times she has been expecting.

The Earth has been a mother many times over, growing and nurturing creatures and plants, filling with new life every spring. No one can say for certain how many times she has done this; her gravid times are innumerable. All we know for certain is that she does it every year, and has since mankind itself was young.

To go fishing in this gravid time, the early spring of late April and early May, is to see her in the first blush of her fertile state. It is the time of the nymph, the bud, the bloom, the early flirtation that will lead to a mate. Everything is new, and showing off its color before progressing to its deep green fullness. Everything is excited and refreshed. The fisherman stands in the stream that still clings to the chill left there by winter, but which is warming day by day to the touch of the leaf-dappled sunlight, and all around there are the sights and sounds and smells of a pagan world wild with the drives of spring.

I went out to fish the other evening, an evening warm and promising a good hatch, the mayflies charmed from the water's surface by the seduction of the first 80 degree day. It was the first evening too hot for chest waders, and attaching the fly to the leader was difficult because my fingers were damp with perspiration and the surrounding humidity. Finding easy access to the creek was still possible, as the weeds and the foliage had not grown up to block the little-used path completely, but new growth foreshadowed an impending obliteration of the easy way in. I was mad for the water, not merely to get a line in, but to savor its coolness in the heat of the early evening.

Anxious to be about the business of fishing, I was still not too rushed to savor the flowering purple things that lined the path, or the new ferns uncurling in the shadows, grateful for what they pledged, both for the evening and for the next few months of warmth and life.

Entering the stream cautiously, knowing that the trout had felt a bit of pressure during the day when other, not-so-duty-bound anglers had hooked work or school to wade this water and put their flies out in the current, I again feel the familiar and pleasant anxiety of wondering if I am sufficiently camouflaged to lull the spooky beings close to my hook. Just as I am beginning to feel too ungainly and foreign to even hope to blend in, a pied-brown sparrow sets down in the water by the stream bank about six feet from where I stand and proceeds to bathe, as carelessly as a baby, in the shallow water. I watch completely delighted, as the bird's presence so close to where I stand encourages me that my fellow streamsiders find nothing threatening or unnatural in my being there. The bird splashes in a delicate but exuberant joy for a long time, and then shakes itself dry and wings off across and up the stream, and I find my heart happy just to have witnessed this little sliver of its life.

I reach down into the clear flow surrounding my feet, and pick up several stones to find out what is there. The undersides of the rocks are loaded with both the larvae and cases of caddis flies. I pull one of the cases off, fascinated with this little structure. This caddis builds its shelter from a silky, sticky stuff like other insects, but weaves minute stones into it, some barely bigger than grains of sand, so that the whole thing is covered over with little pebbles. It is beautiful, really; a little mosaic jewel clinging to the rock. The growing larva inside, tipped with shiny, jet-black beads on either end and the most remarkable chartreuse in the middle, is also distinctively jewel-like and pretty to look at. Fly tiers have tied dozens of variations of both the larva and the case, and I think that there is such a bonanza of caddis on this stream that they must work well. I'll have to sit and do some at the tying table when I get home to bring with me next time.

I sometimes think, when I am here or in the presence of other anglers, that I really should learn the names of the things that surround me. Fly tiers and fishermen who know the Latin name of each species of insect earn my respect, because I have yet to learn many of their colloquial English names.

"What was hatching tonight?"

"Oh, some little brown thingies with sort of silvery wings."

This sort of exchange brings wry grins and serves to reinforce the idea that, when most women speak of insects, a bug by any other name is still a bug. I would like to learn to call these tiny creatures by their given names, just as I would like to learn the names of all the birds and flowers and creeping things and even the fish that surround me on this spring evening. I know them by sight, though, and by habit, just as they know each other, and I comfort myself that maybe I just have a different kind of knowledge that doesn't necessarily conform to the designations given by men. It's a rationalization, yes, but one I can live with and that harms no one.

Some of us were just meant to enjoy things on a less cerebral level… what I am enjoying on this evening is the absolute industriousness of my companions on the water, the way the Earth and its creatures have attacked the job of re-creation with such energy and passion. Every creature but me is busy, and as I roll cast and mend line over and over, casting to rocks and under hanging tree branches, I realize that I am the laziest thing here, even though I am constantly moving. It is as if the trees themselves are straining into the sky, the earth is pushing food into their roots, the insects are feeding the earth with their offal, and the birds are twittering and darting, giving instruction to the whole process. I feel the whole environment pushing up and out, stretching beyond last year's grasp to grow again.

A flaming red cardinal lights deep within the branches of a startlingly green tree. It is the time of crayon box colors, exponentially replicated and charged with life.

Slowly I feel the winter stiffness slipping from me, and I am beginning to feel easy and familiar again, both here in this world and with the rod in my hand. I am beginning to hear the beat that measures the cast, and feel the rhythm of the line as it travels back and forth and shoots from my hand across the water. The current swirls around my legs again, and I feel safer and more agile in its flow with every minute that passes.

It's amazing how much you forget over the winter, like you forget the face of a lover in a long absence, no matter how strong a passion you feel. I never consciously forget how much I love to do this, but sometimes I forget the visceral and emotional reasons why this is so important to me.

Part of the Earth's rebirth is the rebirth within myself, as one of the Earth's creatures, that comes about when I find my way back to the water after a long winter season. I am part of her return to life and her new growth. I feel the hum of fertility and birth in the palms of my hands and the inside of my eyelids, and in the back of my nose, where the smells of new life all around me unfold like flowers in the sun.

How many times has the Earth done this? It matters less to me how many times it has already been accomplished than it does how many more times it will be, at least in my presence, and how often I will be allowed to stand as the midwife's companion as the Earth gives birth to herself again.

Spring 1998

Mary Kuss with a beautiful steelhead.

The Trout of the Year
By Ann McIntosh

I caught my Trout of the Year on a Sunday afternoon in October. My annual fish prize is given for subjective reasons. Any time my skills converge in the face of a number of challenges and I land a big wild trout, that fish becomes a candidate for my Trout of the Year award.

Different waters present separate challenges, so I measure my achievement through a number of comparisons: the size of the fish compared to the size of the water. For example, an eleven-inch brookie taken from one of the small rivulets in the Shenandoah National Park is a trophy, but a bragging-size sea-run brook trout in Quebec must exceed four pounds.

Overcoming extensive angling pressure is another challenge: On the Gunpowder, a well-pounded river near Baltimore, it is often a day's work to get one or two fish over twelve inches to take a fly. Whether or not I catch a fish that has eluded me previously, whether I overcome a new technical obstacle, and whether I catch a fish against multiple odds all factor into the makings of my memorable fish.

That October afternoon I had only a few hours to fish my favorite home water: the Western Run. The water runs through the rural meadows of the Worthington Valley in central Maryland. The farms are showplaces for thoroughbred horses; creosote fences surround pastures studded with mares and foals. When I fish at daybreak in autumn, I hear the music of fox hounds wafting through the dry corn. Murmurs of riders, snorts from steaming horses, the crack of the whip, and the beckon of the huntsman's horn remind me of my fox hunting youth.

The Western Run is a stream that looks as if it should always be shrouded in fine mist. My friend Tom Gamper calls it his "Irish stream," so named for the green of the grass and the "soft" character of many angling days. It is a twenty-foot wide limestone creek filled with wild brown trout—many dinks and a few savvy lunkers. While it boasts bountiful hatches of mayflies and caddis, there are a number of serious obstacles to a streambred trout living a long life. Silt washes down from housing developments in "50-year flood events" that scour the streambed every five years or so; wads of earth cave in when cattle drink from the banks; there are long gaps in stands of shade trees; and poachers abound. Spin fishermen are often seen on the water; they tell me they put their fish back, but I've seen many dead trout in the twelve- to fourteen-inch range hidden under streamside grass. Anytime I have a blank day and no little trout splash at my fly, I'm convinced the poachers have emptied the stream of all fish. I'm relieved if I catch a small trout or two, my faith in the strength of this wild strain restored.

That October afternoon I decided to explore a new stretch of water. Overnight, the weather had fallen from a sunny high of 73 to a drizzly 60. I worried the change in the weather would put the fish off their bite. But, after easing into the water at a horse crossing, I found the fishing was not difficult. In the first hour and a half, I hooked seven trout between eight and eleven inches, all on a #12 Stimulator. I was pleased that the fish were hitting without hesitation.

The wading was tough though, with lots of deep silt between riffles and pools. After slogging along catching fish for a couple of hours, I decided to quit. I came to a dark pool nearly twenty feet long, canopied with sagging maple branches. The water tailed out into a run between steep eroded banks. But at the mouth of the pool, the banks sloped gently, providing an easy exit. "Fish this last pool and leave," I thought, as the mist turned to rain.

The deep water beneath the trees looked so ominous I doubted any trout would come up for a dry fly. Bare roots clogged with leaves secured the far bank and a cluster of three boulders broke water mid-stream. Being lazy, I continued with the Stimulator instead of changing to a deep-water pattern.

I first made a cast upstream, sending the line beneath the branches where it settled down for a good drift. I repeated the cast several times. When nothing happened, I punched the fly harder into a fishy-looking eddy. It was a tough shot. I had to bounce the fly off the far bank. I tugged the bug towards me, slicing it across the top of the water, thinking to change flies. When it neared mid-stream, something gulped the Stimulator, thrashed, and sounded. Startled, I set the hook and was able to keep the line taut as I reeled up the slack at my feet. Once under control, I let the fish run some. Then I pulled and it pulled back—and down. Suddenly there was slack and dead weight. "Damn! It broke me off on a log," I thought, very let down.

But when I tried to dislodge the hook, the fish came alive, swimming downstream and drawing out twenty feet of line like a puppy straining at its leash. This time the retrieve was more difficult and I realized I might be into a Western Run lunker. "Be careful," I thought to myself, getting cautious. "You'll be lucky to get a look at it." I wanted desperately to see the trout and worried it would break me off on a boulder or root before I could tell how big it was.

But this fish turned out to be not particularly energetic. A lethargic lugger, most of the time. I reeled line slowly until I was able to lift the trout to the top of the water, close enough to see. After a few tense moments when I feared the tippet would break, a very large brown rolled on its side. "Good God!" I whooped aloud. The depth and belly of the fish were astonishing, so leviathan in girth that it hardly looked like a trout. In fact, it was a little scary. After a few more short lugs, it came to me at the bank. A lady, I judged, as there was no kype in the jaw. A pregnant lady, I thought, given her belly and the season.

I was breathless, stunned, and so was she. I wound up the rest of my line while she rested, panting in water hardly covering her back, and so damned fat I couldn't get my hand around her. "If she gets away now," I thought, "I've had my look and I landed her." But she was well hooked.

Feeling let down and faintly depressed that the contest had been so short, I dropped to my knees to remove the hook. Now that I had her, I wanted more fight, more play time in the water. I dislodged the fly from the gristle of her jaw.

Measured against my rod, she was a little over seventeen inches long, shorter than I guessed but very heavy. I swore aloud for having forgotten my camera, rocked her in the water, and let her go. Then I stood there, a little sweaty, trying to freeze the moment, bewildered at how essentially indescribable and brief it was.

It was raining hard as I crossed the meadow to my car. As I put away my rod, I dwelled on the fish. What exactly made her so special? Was it her size? Not really, even though this was by far my best fish on the Western Run. Was it that she was so wild, descended from trout stocked fifty years ago? Partly, yes, for there's an exquisite pleasure in hooking and landing a wise old wild trout, especially on one's home stream.

But it was the melancholy that surrounded this trout, I concluded, the miracle of her survival against Olympic challenges, that made her so special. To have reached such girth, she had to have eluded thousands of herons, hundreds of poachers with worms and treble hooks, three or four floods, and God knows what else. As I drove away, I realized how lucky we were, she and I. I had caught her and yet she remained free. I hope she spawned generously and will do so time and again.

Autumn 1998

Cynthia Sarnoski is delighted with her steelhead trout.

Haunted Stream
By Beth Wilson

I go to the stream in the morning, the little stream that very few have found, and push through the brambles and overgrowth to where the sound of water begins. This water is perfect for trout, full of deep pools headed by riffles, undercut banks where the fish can lie in wait for the unsuspecting earthworm or cricket, and fallen trees that provide safe hiding places. This place is cool and shadowy, and so overgrown that the light is dim until midmorning. The sun has not toughened the grass here, and it is velvet thick, the roots having been constantly bathed in the groundwater that emerges into the little stream. In the gloom, it is nearly impossible to attach the tiny fly to the leader, and my fingers feel like monstrous, inept sausages as I squint to find the eye of the hook.

"You have to be patient, girl, or you'll spoil the outing with your frustrated fumbling."

"Don't be so hard on yourself—if you want to use a bigger fly until it gets lighter, then go ahead and tie on a bigger one."

The temptation is there, but I want to start small to avoid a spook, and I explain this to the advocate of the larger fly. I have come in so quietly and carefully, and have spent some precious time just sitting, becoming the grass and the trees and the earthen bank and the bits of sky that peep through the cover, so the trout will not see me as anything other than another part of its world. I do not wish to ruin such an effort by casting a fly that was easy enough to thread but impossible to present with any finesse on a stream this size. I'll take my time and tie on the smaller fly, thanks.

"Soocherself…" I sense a smile and the twinkle of an unseen eye.

Finally the fly is on the leader, and I roll cast under the branches of the trees and around the camouflaging thorn bushes, risking my clothing, skin, eyes and tackle to settle the fly into the water as gently as possible.

"Not bad, but it needed to go a little more upstream. You'll have to cast again sooner than you want to."

"Mind you don't let that fly drag, or all your trouble will be for naught."

Kibitzing, I think. As if the fish don't make me nervous enough, I have kibitzing.

I have brought a cup of coffee with me, and it steams on the bank, waiting for me to drink it and waken my sleepy fingers, so that I don't foul the line or toss the fly up into the branches; but as long as the fly is in the water, I don't dare take my eyes from it. I have spotted a few cautious eddies as hidden fish pass it, watching it for any hint of falsehood. I hold my breath, waiting for the bump.

"Steady... steady now..."

The voices in the wood hush, waiting with me.

The strike comes, and I feel the thrill of seeing it. All catches are good, but to see a fish strike on top of the water at a dry fly includes an angler in the process.

"Nice brown trout."

It is a nice one: about twelve inches long and deep through the chest and belly, golden with large brown spots ringed in red. This one's a keeper; this one is breakfast.

The leaves shuffle in the breeze over my head, and I know that I have disturbed the soul of a die-hard catch and release angler, but I also know that flesh eaten with awareness and gratitude is never consumed in cruelty. This fish will feed my spirit as well as my body, and I am glad for the opportunity to have it be so. I wash the fish, put it in my creel and set the creel in the water where it will stay fresh and cool.

The catch has caused a disturbance in the water, so I decide to sit back for a while and let it settle. I put up the rod and secure the hook, pick up my coffee, and just listen.

"I remember this stretch of this stream from when I was a young man. It's looking poorly now—heck, it's running through an industrial park! This stream used to be deep and cold, full of monster fish. It's silty now, and too wide. This stream is beginning to give in to the ways of man. It's a sorry thing to see."

"I caught my very first trout right here. I was quite a sight: little kid in corduroy knickers with an eight-foot fly rod, crashing around in the thorns, cussing under my breath. It's a wonder that I ever wanted to pick up a rod

again, I was so cold and miserable. But then I caught that little brookie, and I remember being so excited and… awestruck. I was hooked right away, and I spent the rest of my life getting out on the stream as often as I could. It sure does get in the blood, doesn't it?"

I smile at this. Who would have guessed that a woman could feel the same things that the spirits of these men feel? I listen to their voices in the trees, and in the sound of the water on the rocks. They speak to me, these fishermen, and tell me stories of when this wood was full of grouse and pheasant and deer, this stream full of brooks and browns. I feel them here, all around, the anglers and the fish, the hunters and the prey. I am a sensible woman, and do not believe in ghosts. Still, I believe that the natural world has a long memory. I do not find it too long a stretch to believe that these former inhabitants come back to teach those who want to pick up the old habits, and dream of the old days. The love for the rod and the stream and the fish is about all kinds of things, not the least of which is the love for the way the earth used to be. People who love to fish love to be in the places that never forget, that are full of ghosts. They grieve for the foolishness of the world when it cannot stop its mad rush long enough to be told by a forgotten man that you might not have cast far enough upstream to suit you, or that you should forgive yourself if you decide to use a bigger fly because you can't see the small one in the dark.

Summer 1999

Deep Winter
By Margaret B. Clarke

It's New Year's Day, cold, bright, and quiet. There's a lacy rim of ice along the edges of the creek and where spray has splashed onto the rocks it's frozen into a brilliant glaze. Some of the quiet pools and runs are completely ice-locked, open water occurring only where the current is swift. Patches of snow remain along the creekside. Even though the sun's very bright and there's only a slight breeze, the chill's still a penetrating one. Shady areas are bitterly cold, and that makes me grateful to be warmly clad.

This is the time of year to forget the lightweight waders and use the much warmer neoprene pair, as well as at least one heavy wool sweater, expedition-weight shirt and long johns and a comfortably warm jacket. Nothing seems able to keep my feet warm for long once I'm in the water, but I know I'll go on fishing until I can no longer feel them. There's a hand-warmer in my vest pocket, and I know it won't be long before I'm glad it's available. Even though wet fly-line makes for ice-cold hands, I find gloves too clumsy, so it will be good to have the warmer to use frequently.

Dam Pool is frozen over, except for the portion where the water actually flows over the dam into the stream's lower section. There's no sense in spending time staring at the ice, so that means beginning at The Nursery where the water's rushing over the gravel and rocks. A dry fly does absolutely nothing to create any interest in the trout and I begin wondering exactly what the next step should be. There's a patch of snow on the streamside immediately to the left of the first cascade and there are little black specks dotting it. A closer look reveals them to be tiny black stoneflies. Of course there's nothing in the fly box which matches them exactly. The closest pattern in the box is a size 16 Black Martinez nymph, although I have my doubts that it's close enough to the naturals to produce any action from the trout.

The Martinez replaces the dry fly and, no matter that the nymph's by no means an exact match for the natural stoneflies since it's a good bit larger than they are, a rainbow snatches it immediately after it touches the water. That's such a surprise I nearly forget to react, but in this case the body's ahead of the mind and I hook him. He's not large, but he's a grand fighter, still full of spit and vinegar when he's let go. To my complete astonishment, *five more* rainbows succeed him! Then as quickly as the response began, it's over and if there are any other trout in that particular school they seem to think better of trying for the little black bug.

When action ceases in The Nursery and it becomes clear that it's time to move on, the need for the hand-warmer is very apparent. By the time I reach Hemlock Run I'm sure I'll be able to tie on another pattern if it's needed. It turns out the little black nymph is still effective. Even though I don't see any more of the little stoneflies on other snowy areas beside the water, they have to be hatching because two more trout, browns this time, come to take the nymph. There's no doubt these trout are hungry, because they savagely attack the fly before it has a chance to sink very far. Besides the pair I manage to get, there are more than a few hits and misses. Of course, I put down the missed strikes to the fact that being cold makes me clumsy—any excuse will do!—so I don't berate myself for having failed to connect so many times.

Bridge Pool is next on the agenda, but nobody there seems to want the black nymph. The sun's a bit higher now, the air's somewhat less cold, and the change in conditions has its effect. The crowd under the bridge want their flies strictly dry and not too large. Quill Gordons and Dark Hendricksons in size 16 and 18 both work well, and four beautifully-colored, hard-fighting brown trout decide those patterns are just what they want. It doesn't take long, though, for all the commotion to bring home to their neighbors in the pool that something's going on and maybe they'd best let their appetites wait. A few more casts yield nothing and it's plain the time's come to turn around and head for the banks. Water from rain which fell a couple of days ago, plus some snow-melt, have made Bridge Pool a bit deep and swift for comfortable wading, and I decide discretion's the better part of valor and leave the stream.

I draw blanks in each of the pocket water pools on the way up to The Run. The water in those pockets tends to be shallow. It's been truly cold for the past couple of days, so those low-water areas where the air's chill goes clear to the stream bottom may be colder than the trout normally living there prefer. The Run is another story, being faster and deeper than it usually is. The water on the edges is rimmed with ice and it breaks with a tinkling crackle as I step into the current. There are no rises so I debate about replacing the dry patterns with either a nymph or a wet fly. Why, there's a juicy-looking Picket Pin in the box! It hasn't been used in a long time, and perhaps nostalgia makes me decide to give it a try. I make a quartering downstream cast, and as the fly swings it's struck hard.

The trout which has taken the Picket Pin is the one I think of as Big Boy. In this little creek, a 12-incher is a giant, although it wasn't always that way before untreated effluent was allowed to spill into the stream. But Big Boy is in a class all by himself—a 14-inch brown who's been there a few years. We've met before and I'm glad he's still alive and apparently very well indeed. He's as full of fight as ever and the only thing I worry about is playing him overly long and harming him. When I decide enough's enough, I toss him some slack in the hope he'll get off on his own (which would mean I needn't stick my hand into the ice-cold water in which he's living), but that ploy doesn't work. I can see the Picket Pin in his upper lip and decide to slide my fingers down the leader in the hope he'll make a supreme effort to free himself when he sees the hand. That's just what he does, and I'm glad when he's off and gone. We may meet again and I hope he survives the predators he has to avoid. Not many months ago a perfectly formed and beautiful brown trout, a bit smaller than Big Boy, lay dead in the shallow water, a hole driven clear through him. There are two herons in the immediate area, a big blue and a little blue, so it's entirely probable that one of them did him in. So far, the big fellow's managed to escape, and I wish him a long life and plentiful hatches come spring.

Although it would be great to keep going, my fingers are very stiff, hand-warmer or none, and if I didn't see my feet I wouldn't know I had them. The weakness which tells me my body's core is getting chilled has begun setting in, and I realize that can mean trouble. It's far too cold to take the risk of falling into the water because of hypothermia, so much as I'd love to continue, I know it isn't safe to do that. Reluctantly, I reel up and trudge back to the stable yard where my car's waiting. It's been a wonderful morning, a great way to begin a year. I'd come *this* close to staying home and am so happy I changed my mind. It's not often that things go so well, but this time everything came together. Warmer days will come and the fishing can only improve. Even if today had been a completely blank one, it was at least the antidote to what seemed to be becoming a case of terminal cabin fever, and I think all of us need such an escape every so often. For me, the question of when's the best time to go fishing can be answered by: whenever you can manage to get away.

Winter 1999

What The Trout Taught
By Beth Wilson

You are not long in this world before you start figuring out that there are many lessons in life; but it takes a little maturity to realize that not all of them must be learned painfully.

I am forty now, and I must admit that I am having a whole lot more fun learning now than I did when I was twenty. In fact, I wouldn't go back there for anything. I work with young girls that age, and listen to the angst in their voices as they discuss the things that are important to them. I realize that I haven't felt that kind of distress in a very long time, especially not in reference to a few pounds gained or a man slipping away.

The years have put a different view on things, and changed the perspective on what is important enough to rack up blood pressure points over, and what should be approached, not with fatalistic resignation, but a certain clear-eyed acceptance of the *rightness* of what is. When you begin to learn that reality is your friend, and the fact that things are the way they are because that's really the best way for them to be; life and its appended learning becomes more of an interesting puzzle to play with than a booby trap waiting to go off in your unsuspecting face.

This is one of the things that I have learned from trout.

There is probably nothing in the world so unbelievably beautiful, so completely desirable to an angler than a spectacular, feisty trout on the other end of the line. To hold on to that lovely creature, to try to bring him to your hand while knowing that he, at any moment, could snap the hair-like leader with a toss of his sleek head and dart away into the depths of his alien world is a thrill beyond description. Part of the wonder of this is knowing that it is all so chancy: you're dancing with a wild thing, a free thing that you have tethered for a moment, but with a chain that is so fragile and so thin that you can't entirely believe that it will really bind the bursting heart of that creature on the other end. You know, after all, that it is truly the heart of the thing that tugs so furiously in your hands; you know it because you can feel it beating and singing and loving right up your line and down the twanging length of your rod. You fall instantly and completely in love with that dangerous heart, and risk the loss because, although you can only hold onto it for a moment, it is a heart the memory of which will touch yours for the rest of your life, and that is well worth the letting go when the moment of release inevitably comes.

When we think of each other, and the loves that we share, are we really reasonable when we believe that any love is any more secure than that? Don't we learn that love, like catching the trout, requires patience and tenacity and respect and care? Don't we always feel the strongest passion for the one least likely to be tamed? Don't we learn, as time goes by, the needful joy of letting go? Don't we always remember, in the midst of our thankfulness for the one who stayed, the one that got away?

There is a lesson in that.

The trout teaches us to blend in, and to do that we have to consider where we are, and to wake up to it. Looking around, we will see things that we never saw before just so we can learn to look like we belong. Is it so bad to know our environment so well, to notice the nooks and crannies of our existence, that we can fit in if we want to? None of us like to think of ourselves as conformist, I suppose, but there are worse things than knowing ourselves and our surroundings well enough to know how to look natural. Is it conformity or camouflage?

My friend, a very good fishing guide and fly tying expert, says that when you fish where he guides, the water is so clear and the cover so sparse that you'd best go out there and look like a tree. This is interesting, because he is not exactly what you would call a conformist by any stretch, but he is successful because he can blend in when it counts. He catches fish because he has spent so much time thinking about being a tree that you look at him and see a tree. He is tall and lanky, leaning slightly to one side as if he grew on the bank of a stream, and he moves like the wind is blowing him. The lines of his face are like the lines on the face of an oak. His hair curls around his head as if waiting for some nesting songbird to make it home. Most of his clothing is the color of the wood: greens, browns, shadowy blue-blacks and sunny bits of gold. He has become a tree, and it gives him a comforting quality that makes you just love him right off. He and his trout teach that conformity can be a nice thing—it seems, though, that the secret is to always find yourself having to blend into an environment that is beautiful. Never be anyplace where you would be ashamed to fit in.

There is a lesson in that.

There is so much in life that requires our attention, and there are so many of us asleep. The lessons become painful when that inattention gets the better of us, and when life's harsher side takes us by surprise. The trout teaches us to pay attention, because it's rare that you catch him without thinking, and, if you should happen to, the chance is good that he will break away from you before you bring him to hand.

No one can teach lost opportunity like a trout.

Even more important than that is the lesson of the other hazards of inattention. The saddest part of not paying heed is that you miss so much sweetness, so many of the things that could make you happy. All of the anglers I know can tell you which way the wind is blowing at any given time. They not only saw the colors of the sunset last night, but also the ones in the sunrise this morning. They know what phase the moon is in. They know what is blooming, what is hatching, what birds are to be found in what spot and what their song is like. Because all of these things affect their ability to pursue their happiness, they have learned to become aware of all the little things that can add beauty and joy to a life. This perceptiveness bleeds over into other aspects of life as well. Most men who fish can remember the exact color of your eyes, the dimple in your cheek, the color of your favorite dress. Any woman will tell you, this ability is a very important thing to be taught, and any man who has that ability can tell you that it always pays off.

What the trout teaches is not always about trout, or about the pursuit of him. What the trout teaches is how to live, how to calm yourself and hunker down and get comfortable with life. More than anything, the trout has taught me how to feel at ease in the world, just as he does. He is a strange creature, whose world is full of hazards like herons and kingfishers and other, bigger fish and men with rods. But the trout pushes forward, not heedlessly, because inattention would mean his demise, but with the plain perspective that life must be lived fully, even in the midst of those things which would take life away. He spooks, but he also rises—he keeps danger in the corner of his golden eye while looking life straight on.

We live in a sad and dangerous world, and not all of it wishes us well. We are absolutely reasonable to feel spooked, but at the same time we must participate with our whole selves, or we are lost. We can view the more unpleasant aspects of life without taking them to heart, and we can learn from them with as little pain as the trout feels when the hook bites just the corner of his lip, no more than that. He glides away no worse for the wear, and a whole lot wiser.

So can we.

Autumn 1999

Bonefishing in Venezuela
By Catherine Hooper

My trip to Los Roques, Venezuela for a few days of bonefishing in March was the best cure for winter blues. For those of you who followed your husbands or boyfriends or fathers into the sport, I envy you. My husband is not an angler, so I took the trip on my own. Having an excellent English-speaking guide, Felipe Reyes, and an outfitter like Urban Angler in New York is the best asset for this kind of travel.

The first day began with the guide, the boat driver, and I heading out from Gran Roque, the main island, across the dark blue chop and toward the miles of azure flats. I busied myself with sunscreen and bug dope as we bounced across the shallow seas inside the archipelago, and at last we slowed at the beach of a pin-prick island. Felipe, the guide, lumbered up onto the bow of the boat and began muttering in Spanish and giving the boat driver new instructions as he scanned the water. As Felipe explained to me later, a tidal condition he called *reboso* will sometimes churn the sand up from the bottom of the beach as the waves roll in, making the water milky. Of course, neither you nor I would call this water milky—it just lacks the crystalline clarity that is most helpful for spotting bonefish.

Without the *reboso*, the water next to the beach is as clear as a gem lit from the inside. From what I remember from the last trip, you could walk along these beaches and spot and catch bonefish all day long. Unfortunately, the *reboso* stayed around for the entire four days of my trip, so we didn't do much sandy beach fishing. We motored on from there, stopping to wade a few pancake flats where the fish were invisible. The fish were there, of course, doing some fishy equivalent of pointing and laughing. Felipe said that the fishing in Los Roques is tough this time of year because there is more pressure from other anglers. Indeed, we saw two other fishing parties during the trip.

A little discouraged by a fishless morning, we headed out to the last stretch of flats of Los Roques. Felipe gestured past the mangroves as I jumped from the boat, saying, "Out there is the open ocean." I could hear the crash of the sea beyond, and frigate birds hung like kites in the sky above us. We waded across the soft bottom of the flat, careful to drag our feet to scare up any buried rays. And then after about a quarter of a mile, I saw the shadowy glide of a bonefish under the water. Its tail rolled up above the water and winked in the sunlight before it disappeared. I could not have been more excited if I had seen the Loch Ness Monster or the glint of Spanish doubloons. Felipe may have told me what to do next, but I didn't hear him. I cast the line that had been trailing behind me like a forgotten capellini, pulled in a few short strips, and set the hook as soon as I felt the take. After two runs into the backing and a few knuckles popped on my winder, I brought in a pretty silver four pounder with iridescent blue-tipped fins. Felipe was eyeing me with a mix of shock and pride after he released the fish. "I think you have been off catching bonefish without me, Catherine Hooper. You did that like a pro. How did you get so good?" I knew this was the flattery that guides reserve for female beginners, but I grinned anyway.

We walked another quarter mile, relieved that I would not be skunked on my first day out. We chatted politely about our families and the political situations in our countries. And then we saw them: an army of tails slapping the wind. It was breathtaking. We scooted toward the deeper edge of the flat to get the wind at our backs, and then I cast into the congregation. A nibble, no hook. Another cast. Another. Then BAM—and the hooked fish was tearing away from us like a tiny torpedo. After that release, the army of fish (miraculously) hadn't spooked. I caught another bonefish from that school before we decided to stop for a snack.

Although our boat driver was anchored over a half mile away, we heard him starting up the motor as soon as we began to reel up. Although he does not speak English, the driver, Antonio, has the uncanny sense of perception that makes him an excellent guide in his own right. We anchored at the tip of the mangroves, and while we were eating our late afternoon snack, Antonio pointed into the rolling waves in the deeper water and said *"Pez raton!"* (translation: bonefish) I thought he must be mistaken, but indeed I saw something totally new. A school of bonefish was rolling—jumping almost—in the ebbs and swells of the deeper water. They were oblivious to the proximity of our boat as they played, and they were distractingly beautiful. I'm not a sentimental girl, but I was overcome by the thought that they were letting me see something secret about them. And I felt all the more distant from understanding their mysterious power.

The next morning, we chased diving pelicans up and down the beach, climbing over the ropes of tethered fishing boats and throwing our flies into water that boiled with bonefish. The enormous cook at the lodge was getting breakfast ready, and we didn't want to waste a precious 20 minutes of fishing time. Felipe and I were pulling the fish onto the beach and giggling with glee as we let them go. Standing on a wooden boardwalk, I dropped my fly into the water beneath my feet. I had no line stripped out. I didn't even need to cast. I just dangled the leader into the water and moved it by waving the rod tip around. Fish flicked their tails at the fly or followed and then stopped. But at last one fish got hot for the fly and gave chase, interesting every other fish in the school. One grabbed the fly at last and took off, and in my eagerness I tugged the line a little to slow him. Goodbye fish. Luckily, this was the only lost fish of the trip.

After breakfast (and the cook asking us to bring back a big barracuda for him) we motored out to the flats. Felipe insisted, as he had the day before, on trawling this ridiculous yellow tube with vicious hooks as we passed the flats, as he explained, for barracuda. I am not a snob about fly fishing, but I don't know anything about conventional tackle, and trailing this bright yellow noodle just seemed to slow our progress. Felipe insisted that he had hooked three barracuda this way last week, though he didn't land any. Worst of all, Felipe was making me hold the rod. He kept telling me that I had to believe the barracuda were there. I wasn't even interested in catching a barracuda, but I humored him and did my best to believe, as he had asked. The little yellow noodle was streaking through the blue water, and a little smile played my lips as I tried to believe in a big imaginary fish. And then I was bracing my muscles as a grey animal arced up through the waves and pounced on the yellow thing, sending the line screaming through the guides. We hadn't really believed in the barracuda enough to put the top down on the boat, so as it raced around our boat, Felipe would have to take the rod and pass it to me on the other side of the metal braces. The barracuda leapt from the water several times, shaking the sea from its silver-blue body before crashing down again. After ten minutes or so, I brought the fish around to the boat. Antonio and Felipe both had to bring it aboard. They insisted I stay far back, and said that a fish this size still has enough fight left to take off an arm. I don't know about that. As it flopped lamely on the deck, I thought that this was the first fish I had ever kept. It didn't seem right, but it didn't seem wrong either. My chest was swelling with that invincible feeling. Felipe kept shaking his head and smiling. At last he said, "Catherine, this is the biggest barracuda I have ever seen!" When the fish was close to dead, Antonio lifted it and announced solemnly, "18 kilos." Close to 30 pounds! We stopped on a flat to take a picture of me and the fish. Let me just start by saying that barracuda smell terrible. On our first attempt at a picture, Antonio lifted the fish into position and I put my arms out to accept it. Felipe aimed the camera, and as Antonio stepped out of the way at the last second, the fish flopped against me, covering my pants and long shirt with barracuda slime. We all laughed—and I smelled so bad, I had to shed that layer of clothes, and we did it all over again, including the flopping fish. By the time we got the picture, I was down to my bikini and getting scorched by the early afternoon sun.

There's lots more to tell. We saw dozens of rays, some small and the color of sand, some black and the size of manhole covers. There were herons stiff as sentries poised on the flats, a sea turtle floating on the waves like a lost hat. There were small lemon sharks spooking my fish. There was one bonefish that took a fly I had only dropped in the water carelessly as I tried to untangle my legs from the trailing line. There were lots of bruises from getting in and out of the boat, and surgical tape around my stripping fingers. One afternoon, Felipe and I traded casts to tailing fish for two hours as the sun sank into the horizon, neither of us catching anything. There were tarpon rolling off the beach, reminding me of sea monsters on ancient maps. One even grazed my fly with its mouth. And of course there was the charming village where I stayed for the second time. I always say I will climb the lighthouse at the highest point on Gran Roque as I fly over it. But on the ground, that lighthouse never seems very interesting.

Summer 1999

Reasons
By Rabbit Jensen

For a long time, it seems, I was obsessed with the science of fly-fishing. Casting, fly choice, leader design, the merits of different types of lines, where-to-go, and so on. It's slowly dawned on me that this had a lot to do with image, how others perceive me as an angler. Image is not of great importance in the rest of my life, and I've come to the conclusion that it surely has no place in my recreation. After all, how much dignity can one have standing in a puddle wearing rubber pants and waving a stick?

If I just wanted to cast, the plastic casting troughs at a fishing show would do. If I wanted to catch fish, there are plenty of pay-as-you-go ponds. I fish for other reasons. The obvious one is to appreciate the beauties of nature. I once read that the places where land and water meet are sacred; indeed, they do seem to have an elusive attraction I cannot resist. The busy, alien life beneath the water holds endless fascination for me, culminating in the sleek, colorful fish and the eternal puzzle of their lifestyles and motivations. The sounds of birds and lapping water, the smells of greenery and aquatic life, all add their charm. Often I am distracted from fishing by animal tracks on a mud bar, shelf fungi on logs, tiny wildflowers, feeding ducks, soaring hawks, or warbling songbirds. No, not "distracted;" these things are a prime reason I'm out there. I've fished places where motorboats and screaming children were my background song, places where discarded tires and cans were the obstacles one had to steer hooked fish away from, and places where I had to watch my backcast to avoid hooking parked cars, joggers, or equestrians. I still fish such places when pressed for travel time. Mostly, though, I consciously seek remote places to fish, places where I can be at peace watching leaves and drifting clouds while resting the water, without man-made intrusion.

That is the key, I think: Our day-to-day world is artificial, and we feel a vague discomfort severed from our connections to the Earth. I'm especially irritated by the hectic pace of life, everything on a schedule, the emphasis on speed, whether in cars, computers, or even getting a meal. Fishing provides me a welcome relief from hurry, although I admit it always takes awhile for me to slow down from my usual frenzy to the eternal now of nature. I'm not conscious of time when I'm fishing, just a series of events: Hatches begin and end, water flows, the sun creeps across the sky. I'm blissfully suspended in timelessness, a priceless experience in today's world.

Now I'm on a quest to re-discover my angling roots. When I first started fly-fishing, I thought of it as meditation in motion. It was an art more spiritual than technological. I have enough of technology in my job, and it doesn't come easily or naturally to me. I'm more comfortable with feelings: the intangible harmony of the soul, the moment, and the environment. Long ago I discovered fly-fishing naturally leads me to this Zen-like state. When I'm fishing, I become intimately aware of the natural world and my place in it.

One of the lessons I am still learning is that even interruptions in this serene flow are a part of it. Snags, windknots, the need to change flies or position, my chronic awkwardness—it's a challenge to view these as harmonics rather than annoyances. When I do, achieving the nirvana of angling, these petty problems magically vanish, and I meld into the natural loveliness of my surroundings, somehow becoming beautiful myself in the process.

Spring 2000

Trout Morning
By Beth Wilson

Early, so early that the sun has yet to raise her head from under the blanket, so early that she is nothing more than a graceful swell under the green hills, I am up and stumbling to the coffee pot. In the darkness, I bring steaming cups to help us wring the sleep out of our limbs. The bed is still warm, and my lover's body tempts me to find what he hides under the covers, but I am compelled by the call of this morning's cool dimness, and know that there are treasures waiting in the dawn that are fleeting and sweet. We can come back to bed to find each other later; the things we seek in the morning that ask us to rise so early are not so reliable.

We dress in near silence, and this ritual is martial in its seriousness and its exhilaration. Each article of clothing has a meaning, and is chosen carefully for its camouflage, warmth and comfort. The familiar, friendly weight of the vest and boots, the hat brim snugged into the perfect position for shading the eyes; all is in readiness before the tools are chosen. The rod is long and delicate, and suddenly the room seems tiny as the slender but far-reaching rod stretches to the walls. With sleepy fingers we tie the fly to the spiderweb leader.

"What are you using?"

"White Wulff."

"Um. Good choice, I think."

"We'll see."

By the water's edge, we pull on hip boots and fasten them up to our belts. The water rushes by and causes a breeze that is felt low to the ground, barely perceived until an angler leans over to hitch up the hippers. Two pairs of walking boots wait primly on the bank for their wading owners to return to their welcoming dryness, and two expectant anglers enter the stream cautiously, their feet learning about loose rocks and muddy spots and places where the floor of the stream drops off sharply and waits for a heedless ankle to snap. My companion holds my forearm until he is sure that I have found my footing, then releases me to the stream, and I think of how he will do the same thing to the trout, with equal reverence and care, the same gentle grip and the same glad release.

The water rushes and tugs the legs, roaring and whispering persuasively to come along, come along. I look at the trees along the bank, and know that their roots and trailing branches also feel this urgent pull downstream. They, too, stand fast, but it is sweet for all of us to feel the strength of the water and to be part of it. This water has an attribute that the water at home does not have, a cold clarity, a soft minerality that gives it the quality of liquid crystal. A mist rises from it, and blurs the line between water, air, land and human, and I revel in my connection with all that surrounds me. The longer I stay here, the more I am aware that there is no separation between me and this space and all that occupy it.

I cast into the water, carefully feeling the weight of the line as it shoots the fly to the spot that I have deemed most promising. The fly floats, and I can read the water by the way it moves over and through the eddies that crumple the water's surface. Although the downstream current is strong, I see the fly float back upstream on an errant swirl, back toward the small dam where rocks and fallen branches cause the water to tumble in a flurry of foam. I know that the trout love the water right below the dam, for all its violent pounding, as the water there is full of oxygen and food, and I cast my bit of feather and fur into the froth in the hope that my hook's disguise will cause a fish to rise and snatch a meal.

The tree branches above me whisper, *Pay attention, pay attention.*

What is important and what is not changes here. It is far more valuable here to pick up a rock and find it loaded with hellgrammites than it is to know the ins and outs of the stock market. It is critical to notice which way the wind is blowing, what kind of insects are hatching and when, the temperature and clarity of the water, the patterned movement of sunshine and shadow across the water's surface; success or failure hinges on how wise one is regarding these things. Nothing else really matters here, and that is one of the more seductive aspects of this activity. I can't help but think that this reality is more substantial than the one in which I live every day. It is refreshing to be in a place where the priorities are more tangible, even though the results are just as unpredictable. There is no formula for catching fish just as there is no formula for a successful life, but it is much like life in that feelings of success are more about the attitude one brings to a task than the end result. An angler can still have a good day on the stream when he doesn't catch a thing, because fishing is about more than catching fish.

Pay attention.

Fishing is about noticing. Fishing is about heeding the things that one normally does not, but they are the things that make life not just more sane, but richer. It is an attitude that deems it important to watch a white heron take off and wing overhead, or to study the spread of tiny pale blue flowers that are tucked among the greenery on the bank. All of life seems different when it is reflected off the silver surface of the stream, and it is a life that is more joyful and calm, and that makes more sense.

I feel a sharp tug, and it is as if the force of the life on the other end of the line has sent a current of energy straight through the line to my arm. It has happened to me thousands of times, and every time I feel the same breathless, startled joy. Sometimes the tug turns into a wild ride, and other times it vanishes into the pool as quickly as it arose. But every time, I feel the thrill of touching that life, becoming a part of it and sharing a moment of intimacy with it. Although the fish does not want to be caught, there is something strangely non-adversarial in this encounter for me: I am too overwhelmed with respect and love for this life to feel that it is in any way the enemy. I know trout well enough to know that it has allowed me to catch it, that it is less my skill and more its cool grace that has permitted me to find myself with this beautiful, sleek thing on the end of my line.

The fish rolls and twists and shakes, and I struggle to keep the line taut while trying not to horse it in. I feel most satisfied when the fish is barely hooked, and the struggle is tenuous and chancy. I never mind it when the fish comes almost to the hand or the net, and then gives a last toss of the head and disappears into the depths; at least I have had the pleasure of glimpsing it, admiring its gleaming side, and being part of its experience for an intense, heart-racing moment. I like it when I catch a smaller, less experienced fish, knowing that I am training it to the hook, so that it will be more difficult to trick the next time and, with any luck, hold over to be caught again, but not so easily as that first time. It will become a wary fish, needing to be stalked, a trophy requiring skill and concentration.

The release is as gentle as it can be, with wet hands holding the fish lightly as the hook is removed from the corner of the mouth. As this is done, I cannot help but let my attention travel to the shining beauty of the trout itself: the rainbow, with its silvery iridescence and glowing blush, or the brown, buttery yellow with amazing ringed spots. They are perfect and lustrous, gracefully shaped and pulsing with the purest manifestation of life force I have ever felt. The fish is solid muscle, strengthened by the water's current and cold, sanded smooth by Nature's rough but nurturing hand.

I ease the fish back into the stream, letting the water flow through his gills to revive him. I hold him by the tail and gently rock him back and forth, until I feel the tail stir. I let go and watch my prize slip away, back into the stream, going on to roll over more stones for the nymphs underneath, going on to fight the wild water; just going on. A part of me goes back with him; it is the part that wants to live among the rocks and trees, the mist and the water. It is the part that looks downstream at my lover and catches its breath because he is so beautiful standing there, casting intently into the mist, and feels a part of him because we are both a part of the river. It is the part that lifts a few wet and life-laden stones into my pocket, so that I might take them back home, unwilling to let these moments go undocumented.

The water calls me in the morning, and I am convinced that I must listen.

Spring 2000

Faith and Flies
By Mary S. Kuss

It was the summer of 1969, I was 17 and had just gotten my first driver's license. Dr. Donald Pyle, my fly fishing mentor, told me that he very much wanted to take his son Billy fishing up at the Beaverkill, but could not get away from his medical practice. Billy was 10 years old at the time, and already a competent fly fisher. Would I be willing to take Billy up to Roscoe for a week? Doc would pay for everything except my fishing license and meals. Would I! So a week later Doc handed me the keys to his station wagon and his Gulf Oil credit card and off we went. What a great adventure!

I can tell this story now, because I assume there's a statute of limitations on violations of the fishing laws. At least I hope there is; if not, I'm in trouble. It was a sultry mid-August afternoon, the sun high on the water. We had the famous Hendrickson Pool to ourselves; the coming fly fishing boom hadn't yet put more or less permanent crowds on the better-known Catskill streams. Besides, sensible people were having an afternoon siesta to rest up for the evening rise. But with the enthusiasm and energy of youth, we were there to fish, all day, every day. The fish also had more sense than we did; they, at least, seemed to be resting.

Billy was fishing the riffle at the head of the pool, I was about half-way down on the right bank. It had been a long time since either of us had seen any action. In the clear, deep water in front of me I could see huge redhorse suckers, smallmouth bass, and brown trout swimming along the rock ledges. They studiously ignored me and my flies. In the shallows around my feet swam schools of Black-nosed Dace. I'd already tried the appropriate bucktail pattern, results negative.

But now the devil whispered in my ear, and I could not resist. I put on my tiniest fly and quickly caught a dace. Looking through my fly box for something that would serve as a bait hook, my eyes fell on a size 8 Leadwing Coachman. The dressing of the fly was very thin, having seen a lot of hard use—perfect. I soon had it knotted to my tippet and the dace impaled through the lips. I made a gentle underhand lob, swinging the dace out and dropping him into the deep cut at the center of the pool. Soon the dace's struggles attracted an audience of bemused trout that surrounded him in a circle. This was not normal behavior for a dace, but a meal is a meal. After a few tentative nips, a good brown chomped down and was duly hooked.

As I played the trout, Billy called down, "What did you get him on?"

Thinking quickly, I replied, "A Leadwing Coachman."

After releasing the fish, I went back to my flies. I was sure that the fish warden would show up at any moment and arrest me if I kept up the illicit bait fishing, and the anxiety just wasn't worth it. I kept hearing the Sunday School teacher gravely intoning, "Be sure your sins will find you out." I felt terrible. My Catholic friends think they've got the market on guilt cornered, but they've got nothing on the Pentecostals.

A short time later I glanced up to see Billy playing a nice trout. "What did you get him on?" I shouted.

I should have been able to guess the answer: "A Leadwing Coachman."

Autumn 2000

What Fly Should I Use?
By Margaret B. Clarke

Let's suppose that you and I are out on the stream, rigged up and ready to go. The weather's bright and sunny, it isn't too hot and the water temperature's 60 degrees—good for trout fishing. All the conditions seem right, except for two: there are no fish rising and no insects to be seen, either on the water or in the air. How's an angler to know what to do in order to catch a trout?

The first suggestion I have for anyone who'd like really to enjoy time spent fishing is, "Leave your expectations at home. Take your hopes with you, but don't anticipate results of your efforts. Expectations are nothing but disappointments waiting to happen, so don't bother to burden yourself with them." I'd also suggest that if you're going to be fishing a stream unfamiliar to you, you get some information about insect life there from the nearest local fly shop or from a good publication dealing with the waters in that locale. The third suggestion I have is, "Don't ask me." That isn't because I don't want to tell you but is because I very likely know no more than you do. That's the absolute truth; the extent of my knowledge of aquatic insects is abysmally small. Besides that, there's the fact that some of the very small insects are just about invisible to me when they're floating or flying by, so much of the time I simply take a guess which either works out for me or not.

My usual procedure, if I don't get a clue from the surroundings, is to try again the fly I used the last time I was out fishing, provided the pattern was effective. If it didn't work, then it's not likely I'll bother trying it again, at least not at first. There are always what I call the "old standards," such patterns as the Gold-ribbed Hare's Ear, the Pheasant Tail, or the Zug Bug, in the nymph category. The dry flies having a history of success are the Adams, the Light and Dark Hendricksons, the Light and Dark Cahills, and the many caddis patterns, one good one being the X-Caddis and another being the Fluttering Caddis, a Leonard Wright pattern. The Griffith's Gnat is also an excellent choice for a dry fly, largely because it doesn't have a silhouette that's immediately recognizable as an insect. That pattern, as well as the Bivisibles, looks like nothing more than a lot of legs when it's on the stream's surface and that can make it a fairly good attractor pattern. There are so very many fly patterns that trying to memorize all of them would be a task in itself. My hat is off to anyone who can actually do that. Scientific knowledge is definitely a plus and I'd never want to take anything away from someone taking the scientific way of doing things. Still, I've caught my share of trout over the years by pretty well sticking with the "tried-and-true" fly patterns.

If I see absolutely no flies at all, either airborne or floating, my usual choice is a nymph or wet fly. About 90% of a trout's diet is made up of what's under the surface. If you're fishing the stream for the very first time, even if you take the time and trouble to turn over some rocks just to see what you stir up, there's no guarantee that what you find will be what the trout will actually be taking. Take a guess! Tie on a nymph or wet fly and toss it out there. Who knows? Maybe that trout for which you're trying will take it into his pea-sized brain to hit it! Nobody knows for certain what a trout's going to take except the fish itself, and it definitely isn't going to let you in on that. If fish begin to rise and you'd like to use a dry fly, sometimes what can work is an outlandishly large attractor fly, perhaps the Royal Coachman, the Humpy, or perhaps a Wulff pattern. Often using a pattern the fish possibly have never seen before will get you a trout. If all those anglers you know are using minuscule dry flies (and possibly not getting anything), tie on an old-fashioned soft-hackled wet fly, perhaps one never seen at all by modern-day trout, and have at it. Maybe the pattern to use is something you haven't taken from the fly box in some time, perhaps years. Half the fun of fly fishing resides in the mystery.

A couple of years ago I was on my way to the pool I'd decided to fish. One of the members of the fishing club to which I presently belong was in the pool I passed by. He was using a small net to dip insects off the surface and was spending a lot of time scrutinizing what was in its meshes. He then informed me that I must use a size 24 Flying Ant. I thanked him politely and went upstream, saying to myself, "Yeah. Right. I can't even pick up a 24 out of the box, let alone see the thing on the water if I manage to get it tied onto my leader." I wondered at the time just how he truly knew that was what the fish were taking and concluded he'd made an educated guess. He never could have gotten sufficiently near actually to see flying ants going into trout's mouths and I never saw him pump the stomach of a caught fish to see what it had swallowed. He saw flying ants in his dip-net, saw trout feeding and put two and two together. Sometimes you can do that and come up with five.

I got into the pool I wanted to fish, looked around and saw a rise over near the bank. The previous week I'd found a very large dead mayfly on the backlight of my car, peeled it off, taken it home and copied it as best I could, so it was in my fly box. On a whim I decided to try the thing, which was a size 10 (plenty different from a 24!), greased it up and tossed it to the rising trout which immediately grabbed it! I don't know which of us was more surprised, he or I, but I'm betting on myself. After that one, I managed to pick up two more trout, but then they went off the fly and nothing else I tried using did the trick.

It's nice to be given advice, but please remember that's all it is. So far as I've ever been able to determine, nothing about fly fishing is ever cast in stone. Listen to the suggestions, thank the one who's trying to help you, but remember to keep an open mind. Again, no one ever truly knows whether a trout will take a fly until the fish itself snatches the dry fly off the stream's surface or hits a sunken wet fly, nymph, or streamer. What you decide to use may not be what anyone else in the world would employ, but you just may get a very nice surprise—or perhaps you won't. Does it really matter all that much? For me, at least, fishing consists of doing my utmost to catch a fish and doesn't necessarily mean I need to catch one or more every time I'm on a stream.

I hope you and I may fish together one of these days, but if we do, please remember that my knowledge of the bulk of insect life can be found on the front of the Gary Larsen t-shirt called "Know Your Insects." That's the one where the bugs have such names as Charlie, Walt, Bubba, and so on. Tight lines!

Summer 2000

The T-Files
By Rabbit Jensen

"It's a pleasant day for a walk; the sunshine, the running stream…"

"We're not here for pleasure. I have something to show you. Come down to the streamside with me. Now, what do you see?"

"Trees, water…"

"*In* the water."

"Why, nothing. A few specks of debris, maybe some bugs."

"Now, stay as still as you can. And keep an eye on that stream!" *(A few minutes pass by.)*

<GASP!> "A trout! Now, where did that come from?"

"Precisely. Didn't see it swim into that position, did you?"

"No. It just… appeared!" *(The trout in question drifts from side to side, occasionally opening its mouth.)*

"There has to be an explanation. My attention must have wavered for just a split second."

"Shh! Here comes a fisherman. Watch what happens now, and don't take your eyes off that creature for an instant." *(An angler trudges up the opposite bank, pausing from time to time to scan the water. She glances briefly at the pool and continues upstream.)*

"I don't believe it! That trout was there, as solid as you or I, and then it just vanished."

"It will reappear shortly. Just watch."

"It's amazing. Where does it go?"

"I have a theory. I suspect that it travels to another dimension; it can somehow access other space-time continua and transfer its physical self there at will."

"Astounding! There's no precedent in the natural world."

"Not *this* world, anyway." *(Mulder glances significantly upward.)*

"No! That would mean that primitive-looking creature is… intelligent."

"My observations have led me to believe it's far more intelligent than Man, my friend. Or, at least, than *fisher*man." *(The trout rematerializes and resumes its mysterious activities.)*

"Why, trout have infiltrated streams and rivers almost everywhere on Earth! This is a menace The Authorities *can't* ignore."

"What can they do? Our anglers are powerless against these creatures, our deadliest flies ineffective. *(Significant pause.)* Be afraid… be very afraid."

Winter 2000

Flora Soto and her guide kneel to her mighty steelhead.

January
By Beth Wilson

This is the time of seemingly endless night. The drive to work is gloomy, as is the tedious ride home. Long, lazy evenings have disappeared, replaced by quickly descending darkness. I glimpse the first peeps of sunrise, seen so promisingly early in the summer, from the parking lot fifteen minutes before I am supposed to punch in.

This is almost unbearable for the angler with a job.

It is the time to haunt the local fly shops, studying the latest in tinsels and dubbing and bug skins. The fly shop I like to frequent has not expanded its line to include other sports in need of outfitting; when you hang out there, you are hanging out only with fishermen, not buck hunters or duck men. Because this is the case, it is quiet and a bit forlorn in the winter, populated with souls who spend hundreds of dollars on stuff they imagine will make the fish bite when they can't go out and try to make the fish bite. We subvert our lust for the long day on the stream debating the varying qualities of floatant and fingering the beauty of newly stocked Wheatley boxes, peering into their little windows like innocent voyeurs. The lovely and costly rods stand in their rack, and reels, like dark jewels, lie in the folded waves of softly glimmering velvet that lines the glass showcases.

It is beautiful beyond imagining, especially since the fly shop is so warm and dark and friendly. I am understood here, and the sympathetic vibrations of the wooden walls and floors of this place are delightful.

I wander out of the cold, wet parking lot into the local K-Mart. It is January 4th, and the weather is damp but unseasonably warm, so I am heading to the sporting goods section to purchase my new fishing license, *just in case*. The boy behind the counter looks at me as if I am crazy—it is January, after all. It's OK; I am doing this for me. I have been driving around for a week in a panic because, even if the weather turns perfect, even if Joan Wulff calls me on the phone and invites me for a day on the stream with her, I will not be able to go, because the life ran out of my fishing license at midnight on December 31st, and nothing can turn back the clock and breathe the spirit back into it. I follow the familiar steps of the annual ritual, always the same, right down to lying about my weight on the application. I lick the trout stamp and affix it to the face of my new license and imprint my signature across it as required by the state, a little reluctant to obliterate the prettiness of it with a scrawl of ink. The boy in the red K-Mart vest hands me my Summary, and I go home to pore over it and read the names of trout streams, familiar and strange alike, like a litany of sacred places. Those names belong to me again, because I have purchased my license, and I can walk the creek banks without fear of being mistaken for a poacher.

Occasionally, when the obsession overwhelms and the chill air has not reached the point of mind-bending cold, I will dig out my waders and a good heavy sweater and go to the stream, but it is almost always a disappointment. The line freezes to the guides, and the fish sleep under the surface, without the need for food or fight, so the time spent standing in the freezing water is lonely and sad. As the sun begins to vanish in the steely afternoon sky and the frigid surface of the water reflects the winter rays, I cannot help but think about the soft warm pinkness of a summer evening, and the feel of cool dew on bare arms and the salt taste of sweat when I run my tongue over sunburned lips.

There are no mosquitoes in January, but that is about all I can say in favor of the month.

It is the time to sit indoors and read, or tie flies or organize one's boxes, but, most of all, it is the time to feel the longing that comes with being a victim of the seasons, of living in a place where there are times when it is too cold to fish. Maybe if I was more of a die-hard, if I could reasonably see myself sitting on an overturned bucket with a line dangling through a hole in the ice, I would feel happier and less hemmed in by winter. The cold, however, is a harsh and dangerous companion, and I am not yet familiar enough with him to feel comfortable in his brittle company for any longer than an hour or two. That is not nearly long enough to satisfy the craving for the feel of a tug in my hands.

So I dream of warm breeze and cool water and the feel of the fish activated by summer and the hook. I imagine sad Persephone, while I sit by the Vulcanesque form of the furnace, his one eye gleaming red. I let my fingers saunter through my tackle and along the length of my fly line as I clean and dress it in the garage. I comfort myself with the company of fellows, in the dark, hardwood nest of the fly shop or in the pages of good books. I spend time with my fishing magazines, where I can see pictures of bright rainbows and jeweled, dappled browns, and imagine the muscular weight of their bodies in my hand. I study my fishing Summary, and read over and over the lovely names of creeks and streams known and unknown, names that sing the trout song, and meld their watery voices with the music of my dreams.

Winter 2000

Mary Kuss displays her first grilse on a frigid October day.

Panfish Dreams
By Rabbit Jensen

Mid-January. A slow day at work. No windows, posters or photographs relieve the high-tech gloss of the factory. There are not too many places I wouldn't rather be than here. I stare fixedly at my computer screen with a practiced expression of diligent concentration. My mind wanders from automatically calculating the number of days till retirement, and I find myself eighteen years and a hundred and twenty miles away.

My Woolworth hip boots bag around worn bellbottom jeans, the waters of the Lake of the Lilies lapping softly an inch from their tops. The only sounds are the cries of seagulls, the swish of fly line, and the asthmatic rasp of my battered Berkley reel. A variety of ducks splash and glide in the middle of the lake; a vee of wild swans glide silently overhead, coming in for a landing. Fireflies begin their evening light show. I drop my Bitch Creek Nymph in an opening between lily pads. Their serene bobbing is suddenly disturbed as something brushes past their stems, and I strike. My home-built fiberglass rod bends and twitches as I lean back, trying to muscle this fish out of those lily pads. It's an even contest. Finally I begin to gain line as the fish tires, and he swirls at the surface. Another run when he spots me, then a few exhausted flurries as I bring him to hand: eleven inches of almost-black bluegill, a slightly better-than-average fish for this remarkable lake. I admire the lavender highlights from his scales as I work the hook loose to release him. Once again I start casting, confident there are more waiting for me.

Hot sunlight glares from the reservoir's still surface. I stand just within the shade line in two feet of water, sand seeping into my holey sneakers, my cutoffs coolly wet from wading too deep. A bottle of cheap Italian wine bumps against my leg on the end of my otherwise-empty stringer, staying chilled, and I'm pleasantly relaxed from a morning spent fishing and sipping. These mid-day sunfish are wary and uncharacteristically selective. I've had to resort to a #16 Olive Scud on a 7X tippet to tempt even the smallest ones. A long cast away I see the cratered bottom of a spawning area; too far away to make out the ghostly shapes of the redds' occupants. I false cast, then drop the scud delicately between the weed line and the closest nest. My only warning of the take to the sinking scud is a golden flash, and I set the hook. Shortly I land a handful of color: a male pumpkinseed, indignant at being caught, flaring his fins at me belligerently even as I free him. I celebrate the catch with a few swallows of wine: the fruity, slightly astringent taste somehow enhanced by the fishy aroma of the hand tilting the bottle to the sky.

But these images are far in the past. My old tackle is long since retired, and even these cherished fishing spots no longer exist; at least, not as they were. I contemplate more recent memories: an older angler, stout and creaky, but with the same loves, the same enthusiasms.

From the bow of the canoe I spot a heron dipping its bill in the shallows. Its plumage seems grey under lowering clouds. Aft, Mary steers skillfully around gravel bars. She knows the Brandywine better than I, but we both know the honey hole above the dam is not far ahead. Still, there is good fishing all along this stretch, and she drops anchor for a while so we can work our poppers along a deadfall. Scrappy rock bass snatch them, cast after cast. A few raindrops start to fall, and we lift anchor and head for that hotspot. We reach the long, slow pool and I sniff with disdain as Mary rigs up her spinning rod for bass. No 'coffee-grinder' for me; there are big sunnies in this stretch, and if a popper won't tempt them, a Wooly Bugger should. The rain shows no sign of letting up. In fact, it comes down harder, and Mary struggles into her Gore-Tex rain suit. "Where's your rain gear?" she asks. I reply, "You're lookin' at it," and keep on casting. I can't imagine how the fish can see my popper with the rain pelting the surface to foam, but they do. The red popper barely hits the water before bluegills and pumpkinseeds seven inches and up savage it. A fish per cast, and every one a fighting slab of muscle. "You're getting soaked," Mary says. *No shit*, I think but don't dare say. *It's a fair trade for fishing like this!* Rain is coming down like someone had turned on a huge shower. I'm wet through to my panties and shivering, but that just adds a provocative quiver to my popper. "You're going to catch pneumonia," Mary persists. "And it's a good hour to the take-out point even if we paddle the whole way." It's Mary's canoe; even if I'm too fish-happy to be sensible, I can follow the captain's orders. I reel in and pick up my paddle, not without a backwards gaze of regret.

I lived five miles from the Perkiomen for twelve years, and never knew this tiny park existed. Now three of us wade into this long, wide pool, splitting up as if by prearrangement. I'm cool and comfortable in my breathable waders, tackle bag cinched to my waist. My CFO reel purrs as I strip line, and the 5-weight graphite rod is a magic wand in my hand. Two things remain unchanged: the Bitch Creek Nymph on my tippet, and my quarry. Big burly bluegills, with shoulders like piscine longshoremen, their fins edged with neon red, lurk in these dark waters; stronger than their stillwater counterparts because of the effort of working against a current. For variety, there are also smallmouth bass just the right size for light fly-rod sport. It's one of those rare nights when I can do nothing wrong. They are few enough when I'm fly-fishing, I admit, but tonight I hook no trees, and roll-cast the fly free easily the two times I hook an underwater snag. Best of all, that strange telepathic connection between me and the sunnies is operating perfectly. How do I know when one takes my nymph? I have no idea. Their light, quick hits are almost imperceptible when watching the tippet, let alone feeling the strike, and in the murky Perky I certainly don't see them, either before or during the take. Either there's some subliminal cue of which I'm unaware, or my reaction to their hits is totally psychic. Even my casting cooperates. I take fish on the swing, on the dead-drift, even casting upstream. I zing out casts twice my usual length and hook fish at that distance. Every fish but one is solidly hooked, a smallmouth that throws the hook with a last-minute wriggle as I reach to land him. I revel in the sensation of everything going right, doing what I most enjoy and doing it well, until there is barely enough light left to wade out safely.

A coworker pauses at my desk to wish me a safe trip home. "There's four inches of snow on the ground already," she says. "And they're calling for ten before it's over." I return reluctantly from my panfish dreams to the reality of a winter day at work.

Winter 2001

What Started All This?
By Margaret B. Clarke

How does someone begin fly fishing? Probably there are as many ways as there are those of us who take part in the sport. Many of us have learned from a parent, an older sibling, or another relative, while others have been taught by a friend who was a fly fisherman. However it was that we've learned to handle a fly rod, here all of us are, for better or worse, although I'm certain we'd say it's been for the better. I know that's how it's been for me, and one of these days I'd like to know how it's been for the rest of you.

Years ago my husband and I lived in the small community of Pottersville, New Jersey, on premises owned by my husband's employer. We lived in a little brown house set on a green lawn under tall trees, with a pond at the bottom of the slope of the lawn and the river running at the back. When we took the trouble to listen, we could hear the stream chuckling over the stones in its bed and, when I had the time at last to go down to look at it, I found it visually beautiful as well as audibly so.

When we had leisure after having moved in we examined the small red-painted shed across the yard from the house. There was nothing in the shed to speak of, except for one thing: there were several snelled hooks laid out on a shelf which led us to believe the pond down past the lawn contained fish and that the previous tenants had probably fished for them. We therefore decided to try our own luck in the pond, even though we didn't own any fishing tackle. It didn't take my husband long to rig up something and soon each of us was the proud (?) possessor of a literal fishing "pole." Our tackle, if you want to call it that, consisted of a sawed-off broomstick apiece with a hole bored in one end. A piece of sisal twine, some four feet long, was threaded through the hole, with a large knot tied at the upper end to keep the twine from slipping out. Then one of the snelled hooks was attached at the twine's other end and we had tackle, of a sort. We had no floats, but we took the cork from a wine bottle once its contents were finished, cut the cork in half, bored a hole in each piece and tied it to the monofilament of the snelled hook with a piece of heavy thread passed through the hole. We were just about ready to begin to fish.

We had no idea of what to use for bait and, since it was late fall by then, there were few if any earthworms or any sort of insect available. Not to worry; we'd heard from somewhere or other that hatcheries fed liver to the fish they were raising, so on the next trip to market we obtained some. When we decided to try our hands at attempting to catch something out of the pond, each of us had a small amount of raw liver, cut into strips, to use as bait. Talk about disgusting stuff; it was cold, slimy, bloody—utterly repulsive material to use. But it worked! On our first fishing "excursion" each of us caught three fat bluegills and decided we were fishermen.

We weren't satisfied very long with our original primitive tackle. We decided to upgrade things and paid a visit to the local Sears & Roebuck store where each of us purchased a spinning rod, reel, and a red-and-white bobber and began considering ourselves a bit more classy than before. We got quite a bit of use out of the new tackle, although it soon became too chilly for the bluegills, to say nothing of the largemouth bass we were told also lived in the pond, to want to have anything to do with us. We kept on trying to catch the pond's inhabitants, but throughout the fall and winter never got so much as a nibble.

When spring came, the men who belonged to the fishing club leasing the riverfront began showing up. That was my first opportunity to observe people using fly fishing tackle and I spent quite a bit of time down at the river just watching them in action. The grace and precision of the casting, the deftness with which each of the fishermen netted or released his catch, were fascinating. I wondered what it might be like if I were ever to decide to try imitating those I was watching, but theirs was a world I didn't believe I'd ever enter.

I talked quite a bit to my husband about this heretofore unknown method of fishing and also about the beautiful fish the men caught in that way. One day, when the woman who employed him asked whether she could do anything to make our lives in the little house more satisfactory, he suggested she obtain permission from the fishing club for us to fish in the river. She was happy to do so, and one fine Saturday morning a delegation of four members appeared at the door. They told us that the only method of fishing permitted in the club's territory was fly fishing and, upon hearing that, my husband disclaimed any further interest. He'd seen the men fishing from time to time and thought the whole business unnecessarily complicated. He thanked the group and said, "It's not for me."

They turned to me and I expressed a lot of interest in at least making an attempt to use the fly rod and said that although I had no idea how to do so I'd learn. They said that was fine and presented me with a small booklet of the club's regulations, after which they left. They'd probably decided it would be OK to indulge this silly woman who most likely wouldn't ever manage to catch one of their sophisticated trout, and they doubtless had a few chuckles on their way home.

I can't recall where I found the publication in which there was an article about the late Ellis Newman, but I read it avidly. Newman was one of the finest fly casters ever to appear in the Catskill region, and he made the procedure seem, if not utterly simple, at least something I might be able to learn to do. On the following weekend I went over to the local R&S Auto Store and selected a fly rod, reel, line, leader, and a box of large, gaudy flies.

I'll always remember that first fly rod, which wasn't what one could call a refined piece of equipment. It was a gleaming iridescent green, with black-and-white guide wrappings. As I recall, it was about nine feet long and had six guides, and I thought it was just the ticket. It was matched with a Pfleuger Medalist reel and a 7-weight level line. I asked the sales clerk at R&S how to attach the leader to the fly line and he was kind enough to help me out. I could hardly wait to get back home with my prizes and was slightly disappointed when another reading of the article told me that Mr. Newman would in no way have permitted a rank beginner to attach a fly to the leader at the outset. I suppose I'd had the dream of going to the river and hauling in a giant trout, but I decided to play it safe and go along with the suggestions in the article. That meant going down to the bank of the pond, taking the butt and tip sections of the rod apart, and paying out sufficient line to be able to cast it. I followed Newman's instructions and began casting from side to side so as to be able to watch the line. Once I knew how the cast "worked," I again followed the instructions and began backcasting. When that came out well, I put the two sections of the rod together and fairly soon was making halfway decent casts, both overhead and sidearm.

It didn't take more than a couple of hours of trial and error before I was comfortable with casting and decided to risk tying a fly to the leader. Imagine my surprise and delight when I smacked one of my enormous store-bought flies onto the water and a bluegill decided to grab it. He wasn't very large, but his flat sides let him put up a good fight and I realized then and there that fly fishing was nothing like spin-fishing but was ever so much more exciting. I released the bluegill and decided that the next time I decided to go fishing I'd be after the trout in the stream. The first one of those I caught excited me so much I nearly fell into the water, and that happened all over again with the first trout that fell victim to a fly I'd tied with my own hands.

It's been a long road from then until now. It's been an interesting journey from the broomstick, twine, and raw liver bait to the quite-decent Orvis graphite fly rod, CFO III reel, and flies of my own tying. Even though I now have the good fortune to belong to a fishing club which controls fine water, I'll always remember the bluegill pond and those scrappy little fellows. Since I'm pretty much self-taught, I've no doubt some poor casting habits that have developed along the way. Still, I manage to catch my share of trout and other species of fish, and I've never let myself be discouraged because there are plenty of things I don't know how to do. No one who's ever had the experience of fly fishing can ever hope to learn everything about it. All of us are at different stages of knowledge and skill, and the thing to do is learn whatever we can and just do the best of which we're capable. Even in the best angler, the most expert (something I'm not by a long chalk), there's always room for improvement. I believe it's wonderful to learn something I didn't know yesterday, and for me, fly fishing is absolutely grand and glorious fun. It's been a marvelous resource for me and has got me through some very difficult times, as well as allowing me to meet some truly delightful people—like those of you *(DVWFFA members)* with whom I've become acquainted.

I've been very glad indeed on many occasions that I became a member of the DVWFFA and would greatly enjoy learning from others how they began their own fly fishing adventures. Sharing experience and knowledge (or perhaps even lack of the same) can be truly enjoyable, so I hope future editions of *A Woman's Angle* will tell me more about some of the other women in the club and their own beginnings in this marvelous sport. Tight lines to each and every one of you, and may all your hatches be matchable, and your fish eminently catchable!

Spring 2000

Jack's Stonefly
By Beth Wilson

Once a year, in late winter, we get together and tie flies. We pull out our favorite patterns and show each other how to tie them, all the while seducing each other with stories of how well these little beauties work. Some are famous for wild, huge flies with tawdry, multicolored tails of Krystal Flash and great, rolling eyes that glow in the dark, the Las Vegas showgirls of flies. Others tie the tinies, flies that appear to be tied on size 82 hooks, which call for an electron microscope to attach to an impossibly thin leader. It can't actually be determined if the eye of the hook is in fact big enough to exist in this dimension. Tiny flies do not require a fly box: a vacation-sized supply of them can be carried under the thumbnail. These babies must imitate bacteria, but the tiers swear that they work. The question is: does the pattern work, or is its ineffectiveness simply too invisible to perceive? Does the fish hit it, or simply suck it in during the act of breathing?

By the end of the evening, we end up with garish things that look like shrimp that have been birthed in a toxic waste dump ("urban naturals," they could be called), and examples that could only be named "Charlie's Crippled Stillborn Plankton Parachutes."

We had our tying meeting last Monday, and it was during this evening that I was introduced to Jack's Stonefly, and, in the midst of learning the fly, learned a bit of Jack as well.

Jack sits at the table in a pool of light from his tying lamp, the lenses of his magnifying bifocals catching the gleam and obscuring his eyes from the view of observers. Occasionally he looks over the top rim of the glasses at the person he is addressing, and it is then that you see the years of sunlit water that live in his eyes. His face is burnished with the wind and the reflected light, and the lines there are the recollections of smiles and squints brought on by fish and the life that fishing brings to a man. Jack is very tall and slender, but heavy of bone, his wrists and hands big and knotted, clearly strong. His fingers look enormous as they handle the delicate tying tools, but their surprising dexterity and lightness disclose as he works, trimming a feather to exact proportion with a tiny scissor or laying a strip of loose rabbit hair in the fine link of a dubbing loop.

I like to sit next to him as he works, watching the big hand dip in and out of his wooden tying box. He holds treasure in that box, and the faint whiff of mothballs that emits from it does nothing to take away from the appeal of what he has in there. It is too magnificent a thing to dream of touching, but you can peep if you're brave, and there are wonders there that can be seen even without digging. There are beautiful feathers and hanks of deer hair and hare's masks of all colors tucked up among the spools of monocord and the brass tying tools and the jars.

A new fellow asks him, "What do you do when your lacquer dries up?" Jack says, "Throw it away and get some more." The fellow says, "Well, is there a good way to *keep* it from drying up?" "Nope," says Jack. "How do you know when you should get more?" says the fellow. Jack grins and says, "When it's gone."

He knows it's a smartassed answer, but he just can't help himself. He twinkles at the man, letting him know he's being teased.

I think he's a bit embarrassed, and that has helped to provoke the orneriness in him. The man has attempted to extract an expert's secret from him, and his response lets the man know that he has no special power or arcane knowledge influential enough to overcome the natural response of lacquer to air. Jack knows he has a reputation, that there are people who have heard of him and revere him. He's not comfortable with that, and he teases to get people to know that he doesn't want the awe, that he will not allow it, whether he needs to stop the fawning by being brusque or aloof or funny—I've seen him be all three. But his reputation is well earned, and we are sometimes loathe to let it go, whether he accepts the admiration or not.

Jack works the stonefly, weaving on the creamy, butter-colored yarn that will become the stonefly's breast, and then takes a wing feather from a jar of cordovan-colored liquid and dries it. Like the master magician he is, he makes a small split in the tip end of the feather's shaft with a knife, and then peels it down swiftly but carefully. This gets wrapped around the fly, palmered like a hackle, and miraculously the distinct segments of the bug's body appear, perfect in color and that crunchy texture consistent with the exoskeleton of the real insect. What was once a fuzzy piece of fluff is now a leggy, armored beast, no doubt delectable to a fish. But he's not done yet. He builds the wing from a patterned feather shaped with those baby scissors, and the eyes from a bit of floss hardened with cement, and the wing case from a folded plume.

It is perfect. It is so indistinguishable from the real thing that I would swat it were it to get into my house.

This is when I like Jack best, and when he surprises me the most. For all his gruffness, apparent in abundance at times, he is utterly gentle and helpful when he is in the presence of people who are just new, just learning. Last year, at a tying class, my son was having a problem with his fly that he just couldn't seem to manage. From out of nowhere, Jack appeared behind him, and those enormous hands came around from in back of the boy and took hold of the troublesome thing. Jack showed him, with quiet words and slow movements, how to fix it. All hardness left him, all teasing and leg-pulling disappeared. He was patient and kind, as warm as I've ever seen a man with a boy.

He has done the same for me as well.

When you show him the desire to learn, when you give him your attention and your honest interest, there is no secret he won't show you, no lesson he isn't willing to share. The only barter you need make is your time for his skill.

Jack sits back in his chair and stretches his long muscles, and the man asks him if he has a business card. When he opens his battered wallet to see if he has any business cards on him (usually not), there is a black and white picture of a pretty, dark haired woman in there, a picture that was clearly taken decades ago, but a picture displayed so prominently that you know that this is the way he still sees this woman, no matter what time has actually done to her. I think that what Jack knows about time is that you can hold it off, that you can carry things and people you love with you and hold the years at bay, because in your heart and in your mind you are still the true and steady person you always were, and you still cherish the things that used to be more than you fear the things that are. Time is not something that takes away so much as it is something to be given to, to be used to its fullest advantage and filled with all the goodness and devotion that you can give it. With Jack, you cannot say that you don't have the time—time is there for the taking. All you have to do is put your hand to it.

Time is something that you make, for the things that you love and that are important to you, and for him if you want to learn the magic.

He takes the new fly out of the vise and tosses it with a bounce out of his hand and onto the table, as if it were just a scrap, a throw-away. It is a fishing fly, no more, no less, and one that you could learn to tie if you just gave yourself the practice, just the way that you could learn to pull silk scarves out of thin air, if you only had the time.

Winter 2001

Mary Gibney's fly-caught Red Drum.

Priorities
By Rabbit Jensen

A couple of years ago I injured my knee at work. All four tendons were inflamed, and I was confined to a wheelchair for six weeks. No one knows what cabin fever is like unless they've had *that* experience, believe me. I stubbornly refused surgery, insisting that time and rest have their chance at healing me before anyone could stick in a scalpel. Once the swelling was gone and the pain bearable, I started physical therapy in west Allentown, just minutes from the Little Lehigh Creek.

Four good friends took turns driving me to therapy. I graduated to a walker, and begged one of those friends, a non-angler, to drive me to the creek's Special Regulations area one day after therapy. Slowly, with many a pause for rest, I made it to streamside using the walker and gratefully collapsed on the picnic bench there. The sparkling clear water, the fresh light breeze, the smell of greenery, were as familiar and delicious as fine champagne. The deerflies were also familiar, but I was intoxicated enough by my surroundings to accept their presence as a fair trade for my pleasure.

I pointed out several small trout in feeding lies to my friend who, I believe, said she saw them just to be agreeable. Then a good 15-incher emerged from some hiding place and started cruising up the shoreline, feeding on microscopic nymphs, then undulating sideways into the current which would carry him back to the downstream end of his beat, to start again. She couldn't miss *that* fish, so big and brazen was he. I was no less excited than she, despite years of stalking these wary fish.

I didn't recognize that short hour as a turning-point. I made no resolutions, at least not consciously. But in my subconscious I must have realized: I didn't plead to be driven to work to gaze longingly at the factory, nor did I entreat for a visit to the home improvement store where I could contemplate the tools and materials for projects around the house. Unconsciously my mind set priorities, much different ones than I'd followed in recent years, when fishing was something I did only when not busy with or tired from various tasks or my job. In short, once or twice a year. I gave no real thought to this, but in the back of my mind my priorities were being re-evaluated.

I graduated from the walker to a cane, and gradually began setting the cane aside for short walks indoors. At this point, two full months before I discarded the cane entirely, I went on the DVWFFA annual fall outing to Potter County. The other women generously allowed me the pools with easiest access, but even so, it was an exhausting physical challenge in my condition. Even then, I didn't understand the changes in my motivations; didn't consciously realize that I'd discovered the simple truth that fly fishing is important to me.

During the following year I went fishing more often, and caught more fish, than in the previous three years combined. I replaced long-neglected equipment and made plans to acquire more. I re-allotted my vacation time to allow for fishing trips, and established new friendships with fellow anglers through the club and its outings. Looking back, I can finally see how my temporary handicap forced me to examine my lifestyle. Now I can consciously make a resolution: to review my priorities any time I find myself going more than a month without doing some activity, such as fishing, that's a restorative for the soul.

Spring 2001

Steelhead
By Erin Mooney

For what
this bone chilling
numbing cold?

Hard to explain why
harder then, to rationalize.

It is the
catch prize power crown
a pipe from which to
smoke.

The silver pink steel
leviathan
suspended
lurking, lounging
in limbo
waiting for what—
a colorful display, a
sharp twitch of
feather?

We try to guess
that is, after all, part of why we are
here,
why we do this
to understand the
primordial.

The frigid swirl
the interminable day
seeming so
anyway
in the swinging tangle of
loop and hope.

Envisioning
the swerve, the line
alive.

Just twenty feet away
inches, really
from where
I am.
The inches are miles, though.
I can't see it
so, must place inordinate trust in it:
in
the cold
the water
the
fish.

Spring 2001

Mary Bowler takes a bright winter steelhead.

A Fishy Tale
By Judith Palmer

Early in July, I flew to Toledo, Ohio, the nearest airport to my childhood home and where many of my family of origin still reside. I was to spend the week with my oldest sister and brother-in-law who have retired to live in the old farmhouse of my earliest memories. Going back is a wash of affirmation for who I am and a reminder of the affinity I feel for rural life. A walk down their long lane and across the narrow country road provides an enjoyable jaunt to my other sister's house, behind which you can see one of Ohio's true wonders: Sister Sue's half barn. This building embodies such an incredibly twisted and leaning tangle of aged beams and boards, it behooves all who see it to wonder: "How *ever* does it continue to stand?" During this week, both houses bulged and bustled with the return of my sisters' grown children and their children, ranging in age from 1½ to 17.

It was to be a week of work and play and celebration. (Fifty years of marriage and twenty years of living at "the farm" for sister Nora and her husband.) Everyone pitched in to repair cellar doors, chairs, and barn doors; or to tend the large gardens, keep up with the prolific stand of red raspberries, insulate Sue's new garage, or to "bush-hog" the over-grown pasture. The fun part included riding four-wheelers through the twenty-three acres of woods, swimming at Morrison Lake, and gathering around huge bon-fires to visit long into the starry nights.

One of the greatest challenges for me on these occasions is managing to make a meaningful connection with each of these extraordinary family members in such a brief time period. I'm an outsider in many ways, the aunt who has lived in Philadelphia for the past thirty-some years, but yet I'm family. This unique position often means that I am told what those more near at hand may never hear… at least they don't hear it from me, and there-in lies the value.

A small creek meanders through the lower acres of both properties. These woods and creek were my childhood domain. They provided endless fascination and possibilities: if not a tree-house, then a home-made "boat," or maybe a dam; and always there was the fishing and the catching of crayfish. I made my own pole and used a small hook and worms I scavenged from under sundry rocks and boards. When hunger or weariness finally drove me homeward, the cats would greet my return with great anticipation of their feast on my small-fry catch of the day. The fish ranged in size between minnow and eight inches. They were narrow and silver-to-green in color and we called them creek fish.

When I travel to Ohio, I always take my four-piece fly rod with me, as there is good fishing for bass and panfish at Morrison Lake, and the Sandusky River runs within a few miles of the farm. On this visit, I stood on the road where it crosses the creek looking as far up and down the creek's path as woods and course-change would permit. I always come to the bridge to check in with the creek, to savor a moment of re-entry. Every time I find myself coming into myself, re-gathered and whole, standing in the center of all else, with all the universe expanding in all directions from my restated presence. I always belong.

As I gazed at the creek musing about the new generation's use of these beloved woods (I could hear the sound of four-wheeler trails being blazed in the distance at that very moment!), I caught sight of small dimpling in the water's surface. Could that be the little creek fish feeding? How amazing that in all these years I'd never noticed that before.

That evening found me wading the creek, fly rod in hand with a small caddis on my tippet. I had to brave the ceaseless taunting of wise-guy nephews-by-marriage who were convinced there could be no fish in that creek, and even if there were, my gear and preparations surely out-stripped the situation. (Never mind; sometimes you've just got to march to your own drum.) Indeed, creek fish will strike the dry fly, and what they lack in size and fight, they provide in compensatory quickness and trickiness to hook. I had such a good time. Although I know many who read this will completely understand my endeavor on that lovely soft summer evening, at one point I laughed out loud to imagine other anglers giving witness to this outing… and I was glad to be out of sight from the road. But then, who would even think to look!?

And so it was that I marked the reunion of my 56-year-old self with my 8-year-old self: enjoying the golden rays of the setting sun which made my creek look more beautiful than I'd remembered it, happily fishing my first home waters.

Autumn 2001

The Bamboo Perversion
By Rabbit Jensen

A convoy of shiny vehicles bounced slowly down the dirt road amidst clumps of hemlock and rhododendron. In a clearing, several deer stood agaze, ears swiveling, before springing into the shrubbery. At last the cars reached a parking lot and pulled in, one by one. My red Ford pickup, at the end of the row, looked like a draft horse tethered in a line of thoroughbreds. At least it was nicely polished; what I love, I love.

Eight women gathered around a rustic picnic table, eating lunch and discussing tactics. I savored my sharp cheddar cheese; no faddish foreign cheeses for me. A simple taste, like my pickup truck. I joined the discussion, asking to be in the group going to the most remote stretch of stream.

Lunch finished, three of us left for the farthest parking area. Once there, the others eagerly geared up, alternately teasing me for my characteristic slowness and urging me to move faster. I would not be rushed through my methodical routine: first the mat to protect my stocking-foot waders from abrasion; the socks, meticulously smoothed; the waders themselves, then the careful donning of the wading shoes, assuring the bulky neoprene feet were smooth inside them. The gravel guards hooked and velcroed in place, then standing to adjust the shoulder straps and put on the wading belt, after distributing the various lanyards, pouches, and D-rings around its circumference. Rummaging through a pouch to find three types of sunscreen and a bug repellant, all applied with great care.

By now my companions were dancing with impatience. "I'll catch you up," I said, and they were off down the trail like dogs let off the leash. I shrugged into my vest, and pulled a reel case out of the bottom of my tote bag: an old Hardy Perfect, which emitted a well-bred purr as I stripped out the leader and ran it through my rubber straightener. Furtively I glanced around to make sure no one saw me pull a rod tube from behind the truck seats. Unscrewing the cap, I slid out two sections and laid them gently on the seat: faceted like six-sided jewels, the color of topaz. From an inner vest pocket I pulled a Ziploc bag, extracting Q-tips and a clean rag to wipe the already-immaculate metal ferrules, applied a special lubricant, then I fitted them together with all the care of a watchmaker. No one saw me caress the golden cane surface before I seated the Hardy, then ritualistically strung the line through the guides, admiring each inch of my bamboo jewel as I did so. What fly? A little puff of deer hair and dubbing designed to dance the water's surface.

I acknowledged the greetings of my fellows as I walked past on the trail, but didn't linger long. They didn't notice my bamboo sweetheart held behind me, out of casual danger, out of their sight. At last, far from prying eyes, I found a lovely ledgerock pool, the perfect setting for my jewel. A few false casts washed away the muscle-memory of graphite, and my arm muscles remembered the slow firm stroke that brings life to a split cane rod. Golden highlights flashed in the sunlight, the little dry fly wafted through the air and settled to the water with the grace of dandelion fluff, shyly offering itself to the trout like a teenage girl hoping for a kiss on her first date. Perhaps it's just my imagination that a bamboo rod presents a dry fly more delicately than any other. If so, remember that in fly-fishing, confidence is the key. I believe it, so for me, it happens. And, there I was, just me and my sweetie, sharing the passion and poetry of fly-fishing.

Not for me the no-nonsense bottom-dredging that was working for the others. I shudder at the thought of flinging weight with my darling cane. That's not the job it was crafted for. Gossamer dry flies and tiny wet flies, fur and feather creations as natural and lovingly made as that bamboo rod. An organic connection, from me through the living cane, down the line and leader to the fly, hackles breathing in the sparkling current. Sometimes I wonder what it was like two decades before my time: Did silk lines and gut leaders complete that connection, have a feel that modern synthetics don't?

I caught a couple of fish that afternoon, bright and lively streambred browns with a subtle beauty matching the rod that subdued them. The important thing, though, was the poetry of the experience: the hand-crafted golden beauty of split cane, delicately wafting a dry fly onto water as clean and clear as when the world was new; the subtle rise of a native brook trout or streambred brown, then the primeval struggle of prey and predator; the prey lovingly released, like the kiss after passion's satisfaction. And that's just what it is, my grand passion.

Why do I love bamboo? My graphite rods throw a tighter loop, are more durable, take more abuse. They are production-line tools easily replaced if I damage them or wear them out. Heaven knows they're cheaper than cane. And I don't hesitate to use them to fling huge poppers or Wooly Buggers, stalk big bass in complex cover, or fish urban streams with surfaces swirling with unknown chemicals.

Why do I love bamboo? Is it that I'm such an individualist I relate to a rod that is hand-crafted, from selection of wood to varnishing the guide wraps? Is it a symbol of a simpler time, a link to a past as golden as the cane itself? Is it the same atavism that draws me to acoustic music, old books, archaeology, and a lifestyle more suited to 1940 than 2002?

I'm not an investor; none of my cane rods have names that command five-figure prices. It's how they felt when I first handled them, cast them, that whispered "Buy me." I'm obviously not out to impress people. In fact, I'm almost fanatical in seeking remote, lonely places to share with my lovely six-sided darlings. And there is the clue.

Why do I love bamboo? I'm a pervert. I want it all to myself, from the first topaz gleam when I open the rod tube, to the final loving caress as I wipe moisture from the satiny cane before sacking it at the end of the day. No prying questions or jealous glances. Above all, I don't want to feel obligated to tell someone, "Here, try a few casts." This is *mine.* I'm as possessive as a two-year-old, as greedy as a miser, as compulsive as an addict. Addicted to a timeless beauty I can feel as well as see.

But I'm a happy pervert, possibly even a well-adjusted one. The only change I plan to make is to acquire more bamboo rods to cherish. To quote Diana Ross: "If there's a cure for this, I don't want it."

Summer 2002

Rabbit Jensen catches most of her trout using a split-bamboo rod.

Retreat
By Elayne B. Howard

I walk the paved parking lot with wavy heat radiating
up from the blacktop onto my damp back.
I step onto the path of cedar wood chips, and
face the coolness of the shaded woods.
I pause. I close my eyes and inhale the scent of the
moment, dominated by the fragrance of cedar.
I sense the serenity of the calling chirps of
birds answered by fluttering wings,
and I know all is right—the peaceful light enters my soul.

Then, my steps crunch along the trail as I see the
death and falling of the once-live, jade leaves.
The browned foliage is remnants of yesterday;
I release the memory to the light.
I hear a scurry of crunching off the path as squirrels
scarf up kernels for the coming cold.
I feel the seeds and leaves tap my face in the swirling breeze,
and I know all is right—the sun is behind the clouds.

Then, I leave impressions of my feet in the freezing blanket of white.
Hairs tickle my nose as I breathe in the air, and
I smoke the space when I exhale.
Cold burns of snow skim down and flame my
cheek as I brush against weighted shrub.
I squint in the shimmering reflections of the clear sky light,
and I know all is right—I am part of the air.

Then, I awake to the light and the serenade of
birds, recalling that welcomed refrain.
My eyes rise to the bushes and trees above yesterday's leaves.
I stop to stroke the green buds, the frontier of tomorrow.

I nearly taste the receding smell of damp decay, mingled
with the new fragrance of fresh renewal,
and I know that all is right—I am part of the peaceful growth.

With lighter steps and breaths of fresh air, I retreat towards my car.
The reflection in the lake snags my eye, and I must
stop for the water to reveal the familiarity.
I recognize myself, but soft ripples are smoothed by
glassy water to unveil the year's maturation:
a new crease, a few silvery strands, and more inner strength to follow the
moments of my lineal life blended with nature's cycles and longevity.
And I know that all is right.

Summer 2001

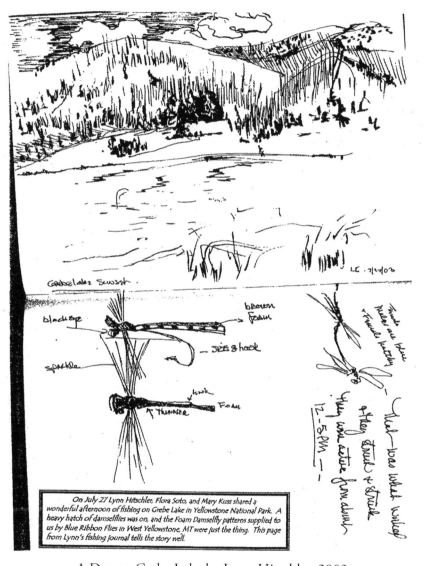

On July 27 Lynn Hitschler, Flora Soto, and Mary Kuss shared a
wonderful afternoon of fishing on Grebe Lake in Yellowstone National Park. A
heavy hatch of damselflies was on, and the Foam Damselfly patterns supplied to
us by Blue Ribbon Flies in West Yellowstone, MT were just the thing. This page
from Lynn's fishing journal tells the story well.

A Day on Grebe Lake by Lynn Hitschler, 2003

Witching Hour
By Margaret B. Clarke

It's seven o'clock on a late summer evening and all's fairly quiet. The commuter traffic out on the road has gone, the sheep and horses have been put away, fed and watered, and now the creek meadow and the upper reaches are all mine. This is really my favorite time of day to fish because the brightest light has gone, the air's beginning to cool, and I know the trout will soon begin stirring from their various daytime lies. The mayfly hatches are mostly gone and there aren't many caddis about, but terrestrials remain active and probably will be so until well into autumn. Even if the land insects weren't still fairly abundant, the stream always harbors nymphs. There are crayfish here, too, although many of those I've seen have been too large for the average trout living here to manage to eat. They probably can get the smaller crayfish and very likely do eat them. I can be reasonably sure about that because once I used a crayfish imitation and managed to pick up a trout with it.

In a little over an hour it will be full dark, so it's time to hurry over to the stream and start fishing. Arriving at precisely the right time for good fishing involves a little calculating: get here too early and there's nothing happening; come too late and it's then too dark to wade among the rocks without a lot of stumbling around. Even in a stream I know as well as this one, the picture alters dramatically with darkness and I've broken all the bones I care to break in this lifetime. There's also the matter of being able to see what I'm doing in order to remove a fly gently and safely from a trout's mouth when releasing the fish. But in the short time available to engage in it, for me there's nothing like fishing at eventide.

It's been some time since I tried the upper portion of the creek, so I walk up to The Run. That area's a bit different now, because the bank immediately below that piece of water has been reinforced with rocks to prevent further erosion of the soil. That makes for a stretch of current that's not only a good bit deeper but a lot swifter, and I lack the daring to venture into it. I therefore stick to the bank, fighting my way through the barberry and multiflora rose bushes as I approach the waterside. When at last I get near the edge of the stream, I stand and simply watch.

There! A rise-form appears, so there's a fish feeding. It might be a chub or a small suckerfish, but somehow I don't believe it's not a trout. What can it be taking? Did it suck in a floating beetle or ant? Whatever it was, it didn't make a lot of fuss and a grasshopper that fell into the stream would cause a commotion, but nothing of the sort happened. I decide to bet on a beetle imitation and dig one from the fly box, attaching it to the leader. That takes a little doing because the light's beginning to fade and the fly is a size 16. In order to see the hook's eye, I have to hold the fly up to the sky so as to be able to aim the tip of the leader properly. At last the beetle's on and I'm set to cast.

The first rise is followed by another, then by two more. I decide to start with the riser closest to where I'm standing and drop the fly onto the surface, leaving enough slack in the fly line to ensure at least some drag-free drift time. When the beetle reaches what seems to be the "ball-park" the trout rises again—next to the fly. I want very much to pick it up and cast again but know I'll have to wait and let the current carry the fly, leader and line out of the trout's immediate range of vision or I'll put it down. It's hard for me to be patient when fish are obviously feeding, but to try to hurry things means I'll probably scare everything in the pool and catch nothing.

As the light continues to dim the water reveals more activity. There are trout rising all over the place, seeming almost to try to shove each other out of the way as they feed on whatever it is they're taking. Between the approaching dusk and the size of the trout's prey, I can't be sure of what that may be, but I stick with the beetle and send it out to them once more, keeping my eyes fixed on the end of the fly line. The line stops moving. It's a very subtle take, if that's indeed what it is, but I take no chances and strike. The trout, which is very small, leaps out of the water and seems almost to fly closer to the bank. He's probably not longer than six inches, but he fights hard enough to put a bend in the rod.

As quickly as I can, I draw him over to where it's possible to reach and release him. Yes, he is a little one and he has the beetle in the corner of his mouth. I know that using the forceps will make it easier to get hold of the fly and take it out, so I hold him in the quiet current near the stream's edge while opening the tool. I tuck the rod under my arm, reach down and take the trout by his lower lip with my rod hand, putting the forceps on the hook's bend. Just before removing the fly from my quarry's mouth I take a moment to admire him. He's lovely—dark golden-brown, brilliantly yellow just above his snow-white belly. All over his sides are black spots, interspersed with red ones, and his fins and tail have taken on the red-spotted deep amber of the stream-bred fish. After a very short time spent in enjoying his beauty, I slide the fly carefully from his mouth and send him on his way.

When he's gone I decide to stay for just another short while. It's going to be dark soon and I know I'd do well to leave. But the magic of the evening has caught me and despite my better judgment I cast again above where a rise-ring has appeared. There's no take and I know that the trout has either ignored the fly or I've misjudged the fish's location altogether. In the short time it took to get the cast off it's become even darker and I'd really be wise to leave. "One more cast," I tell myself. "Just one more." Fortunately, since there aren't enough insects in the air to attract the bats, there's no danger of my snagging one of them or of having the "winged mouse" bounce off the tip of the rod. I peer hard at the stream's surface and am barely able to discern a large rise-ring and cast above and to one side of it.

At first there's nothing, but then there's a splash marked by a whiteness on the surface and a hard tug on the beetle. I've got him! As the trout surges against the pressure of the rod, I realize that releasing it isn't going to be easy because now I can scarcely see what I'm doing. The fish fights hard, thrashing about in the water, darting this way and that in the effort to escape. It's then that I begin to wonder exactly how I intend releasing him when he's ready to stop struggling. I don't get the chance to consider the problem for long because there's one last hard pull and then nothing. The arc's gone from the rod, there's no more splashing, and I wonder just what's happened.

It finally occurs to me that on the key-ring in my vest pocket is a small light. I dig into the pocket, get hold of the ring and turn on the light, shining it around. The mystery is solved because I can see that I'm near a partly submerged fallen tree. My trout very probably made for the tree, wrapping the leader around a protruding branch and freeing itself by snapping the fine tippet. I'm sorry he's gone, even though I'd have released

94

him anyway. It would have been gratifying to see him, to know whether his size was commensurate with the fight he gave me, but he didn't wait around once he knew he was loose.

My last excuse for hanging around is gone because it's far too dark to tie on another fly. I reel in the fly line and decide to check the leader. When I hold it up to the flashlight's beam and examine it, I'm relieved to find that most of the tippet is still there. That means the trout seems to have broken off the fly immediately above the knot. Since the fly's a small one and is barbless, he'll no doubt be able to rub it out without difficulty. He also won't need to contend with a long piece of leader that could trap him later. Maybe we'll meet again, if I'm lucky, so on that thought I decide to leave.

Once the fly line is back on the reel, I make my way back to the car, keeping the beam of the light on the path and walking with care. It doesn't take long to reach the car, put the rod and reel back into their cases and take off my gear. When all that has been done, I take time to look up at the sky. It's a clear night, there are what look like a million stars overhead and before long the moon will rise. Just before I get into the car I walk over to the bridge and look down at the stream. The stars shine on the water, their reflections broken up by the constant making of rise-rings. The trout are truly "on the feed" now, and if it were just a bit lighter I might give in to the temptation to stay. But discretion overcomes that wish and I turn back, knowing that the stream will be there next time I come out. Fishing in the near-dusk has its own very special sort of magic, enough to cause me to think of that short time before dark as "the witching hour." For me it is, because the experience of being out on the stream and finding it so hard to leave is close indeed to being under a spell, completely bewitched.

Summer 2001

Stages of a Fly-Tier
By Rabbit Jensen

I started tying flies before I started fishing. This peculiar reversal has affected my entire attitude towards fishing. In a sense, fishing is a testing ground for my fly-tying creations as much as it is an activity I do for its own sake.

When I was in college, my desk was permanently set up for fly-tying and I'd study sprawled across the bed. When studying became tedious, I'd stop and tie a fly. Seldom the same one twice; I had pages of flies from the Orvis catalog hung on the wall as samples, and well-worn copies of pattern books and "Fly Fisherman" magazine. I'd pick a fly that caught my eye and tie it. My fly boxes were filled with classic streamers, attractor wet flies, scaled-down steelhead flies, and big bushy dries. This is what I call the Standard Pattern Stage of fly-tying, when every fly in the box has a name.

Of course, tying such a wide variety of fly types was a wonderful excuse for buying materials. And in every order, I'd have one item that was just a whim. Who could resist that striped chenille? Or the sparkly yarn stuff? Oddly shaped hooks touted as weedless? "Floss grab bag, ten spools for $1.00." They pick the colors, but who can pass up a bargain like that? So, I had to do something with the royal purple chenille and the school-bus yellow deer hair. I call this the Wild Pattern Stage. "How would this Adams look with a bright orange body? How 'bout I tie a Black Ant, only make it Kelly green?" I seldom actually fished with the results of these experiments. I was confident any self-respecting fish would levitate out of the water to avoid any one of them. Oddly, I retain this attitude, despite the fact that some of these pop-art-sculptures-on-hooks have been amazingly successful fish-catchers. Sadly, I tied flies far more often than I fished with them, or I would have learned to appreciate the value of these attractor patterns.

As I read books and magazines, I gradually became aware that there was a phenomenon called Matching the Hatch. Now, that sounded really interesting. I love puzzles; I enjoy tying flies. Here was a grand puzzle: figure out what the trout are feeding on and tie a fly to match it. At first, I fell back on the Standard Patterns, carefully studying the succession of hatches and tying classic Catskill dry flies. A few jaunts to well-known waters during peak Mayfly hatches, and I realized I was on to something a whole lot of fun. I expanded my knowledge (and bought more fly boxes), including terrestrials and nymphs. This is the Hatch-Follower Stage.

At that time, nymph-fishing was a fairly new technique and there were few standard patterns. Instead, there were "styles" of nymphs, each with the same basic parts but using different colors and proportions to match the desired insect. This made me aware of a whole new challenge: observing my local insects and designing my own flies to match them. At first it was variations on Skues-style or Rosborough-style nymphs. Then one day I observed a nymph hatching on a rock, and it wasn't really shaped like either one. I went home and tied a shaggy grey cigar-shape ribbed with maroon floss, and caught a brook trout on it the next day. What a feeling of accomplishment!

This began the Hatch-Matcher Stage of tying. I had found an art I could truly immerse myself in. I studied the works of the masters, not for specific patterns, but for tying techniques. I laboriously sounded out the Latin names of insects as I studied their colors and proportions in heavy tomes full of enlarged photographs. I set up my tying desk next to a window so I could view my materials under natural light. I'd pick a pinch of dubbing from my palette of colors, squint at it as I held it with the sun behind it, adding just a bit of another color, a few fibers of a third, until the blend satisfied my artistic sensibilities. I cultivated a sparse hand at tying, to make my creations seem more fragile and insect-like. I lauded the virtues of natural furs and feathers, with their variations of colors, so suggestive of the illusion of life and motion. I tried to evoke this motion with soft waving hackle, long guard hairs, wisps of marabou. I could have become the type of tyer that counts the gills along a nymph's abdomen and ties in exactly that many hackle tips. Instead I chose Impressionism, and adhere to this scholia to this day. My flies suggest, tantalize the fish with a promise of something tasty. Of course, this means I can hardly show my fly boxes to others, and have no clear answer when asked, "What did you get him on?" Something grey, with a come-hither halo of gamebird hackle, fished just under the surface. "A grey emerger" is the best I can do.

As Life imitates Art, and Art imitates Life, my art-on-a-hook has molded my fishing methods. When I cast a fly, my aim is to introduce it delicately to the water, present it to the fish with the subtlety and savoir-faire of a waiter placing the specialté-de-maison before a discerning diner. Any great chef knows that fine food deserves proper presentation. I serve my flies on a long, fine leader, after the most careful of approaches. All I ask is the appreciation of my intended audience, the trout, expressed by eating my piece-de-resistance. And if they turn up their aristocratic snouts at it, I secretly revel in their incredible selectivity, and delight at the ever-new puzzle of just how to tempt their sophisticated palates.

Just as I attain this artistic Nirvana, invariably, some far more practical angler comes along and lobs an attractor fly into the pool: a Royal Wulff, an Irresistible, a Wooly Bugger, or, heaven help us, a Green Weenie or San Juan Worm. The trout turn on like they've been waiting all their lives for this thing. It's like a brick heaved through my work of art. I feel disillusioned, betrayed, insulted. How dare these creatures with their pea-sized brains spurn my masterpiece, and crawl all over that... that... neon sign! It's like pushing aside a Filet Mignon to devour a Big Mac. The angler moves on, having caught and released more trout in ten minutes than I have all morning. I sigh, cut back my leader to 5X, and start rooting through my fly boxes. Now where did I put those black-and-chartreuse wet flies with the hot pink hackle?

Winter 2002

Downsizing
By Ralph "Jake" Jacobsen

Christmas was good last year. The boys, 23 and 21, were great. They actually remained in an upright position for extended periods of time and even spoke. For the uninitiated, the default here is always the horizontal position and vocabulary is limited to "duh," "nowhere," and "sure." Yes, by the way, this position can even be maintained on a piano stool. I was feeling especially prosperous and gave my wife a new Filson strap vest, the Scientific Anglers waterproof fly box with removable inserts, and a neat bunch of nymphs. The logic being simplify, downsize.

Time passes. It is now April, opening day for trout has passed, and after many gentle but persistent reminders, the moment of truth is about to arrive. This "moment" consists of the switchover of flies to the new box and gear to the new vest. The Saturday before our annual pilgrimage to Potter County, the games begin in earnest. Stage One should be easy. Remove the contents from the old fly boxes and place them into the new one. Understand, this new Scientific Anglers box is about 7 3/4" X 4 1/2" and, depending on the inserts you select, can hold over three hundred flies without even a hiccup. 10:00 a.m. and the table is covered with boxes and flies. 11:30 a.m. and there is mumbling and the mention of wine. It's only 11:30, I must have misunderstood. "Honey? Are you okay? Everything all right?"

After twenty-six years of marriage I now know to finally listen to that little voice when it says to go shop for car wax. I leave and return two hours later to find the scenery on the table has remained but been rearranged. There is also a large, half empty bottle of Chardonnay. Realizing the car wax routine cannot be used more than once a day, I face the demon head on and ask how it's going. To this very day I swear I heard a hiss before she spoke. She explained this was far more complicated than I was capable of understanding. One needed to identify each of the flies by name, size, type and function. She also explained this becomes difficult when you have over twelve years of accumulated "things" which have their origins from Pennsylvania to Branson, Montana. I chuckled and reminded her some of these "things" don't have names and that she bought them because they were cute. Yes I know, and before you say it, I really did wish I could take those words back.

4:00 p.m. and I now realize this is a matter which transcends jewelry, clothes, even shoes. 5:00 p.m. and I make dinner. One person in the house is not hungry. 7:30 p.m., her eyes are closing and the bottle of wine is almost empty. Sensing weakness, I propose a plan. Wets, dries, similar looks and then by size. She's too weak to fight it. It's done: the Scientific Anglers and an extra box for streamers.

Sunday begins at 8:00 a.m. and someone has a headache. Hmmmm. The good/bad news is it's Sunday and we have no wine. Church is mentioned, and I am presented with the logic of "the closest distance between two points," AKA prayer, is just as good. Okay... There is a lot of pacing. By 9:30 the old vest is brought out and emptied. Our family room is 16 by 34 and all of it is utilized. The contents of her vest are formidable. I see things I remember and smile. I see things I don't remember and some things I still can't identify. No less than five flashlights, two thermometers and seven spools of 4X tippet are revealed. I remain silent however, as I already have eight cans of car wax. The Filson is a great vest. Two large pockets along with 6 smaller external ones and four internal ones. What sets it apart is the double back pack sections and it is a strap vest. This is NOT the 438-pocket Orvis vest she is used to. I offer encouragement by saying she has eliminated four fly boxes, and suggest only one flashlight, thermometer and so on. Once again there is the mention of wine. 2:30 and the pockets are bulging!

There are still six square feet of "things" on the floor and that's not counting the net, wading staff, water bottle and rain gear. She tries the vest on in front of a mirror, returns to the room, empties the new vest and within ten minutes, has the old Orvis re-packed. "Here! You like it so d@#$ much, you try it." She leaves to go across the street and tells me she is going to celebrate the re-birth of her old vest. I guess they have wine.

It is now 7:00 p.m. Thursday night and I have my old fly boxes out and the contents of my old vest on the floor. There is a bottle of scotch on the table and she has informed me she has to go out to look for shower curtain rings. Funny... I swore we had extras already. Wish me luck.

Summer 2002

Home Waters
By Rabbit Jensen

When I first started fly-fishing, I had no car and little money. At college in Pennsylvania, I bummed rides to Ridley Creek. Summers in South Jersey, I was limited to waters within bicycle range, except for rare days I could beg my dad's car. That meant I fished The Pits, an old quarry turned into a village park, and sometimes the local reservoir. I fished these waters at least once a week, all year 'round, for several years. Therefore I got to know them more thoroughly than any fishing spot since.

There's something about knowing a piece of water this intimately. It's a love relationship like a long-standing marriage, soothingly predictable but always evolving. It's as comfortable and comforting as a well-worn pair of jeans; nurturing, soul-soothing, a center of serenity, like an easy chair and a box of chocolates after a stressful day. Lacking the need to read new water, plan approaches, locate fish, or find access points, I found I'd reach my beloved fishing spot and just fall naturally into its rhythm, no conscious thought needed or wanted. Sheer familiarity with those favorite waters quelled my novice insecurity and introduced me to the angler's Zen state. To me, that intimacy is a major part of fly-fishing's charm.

That's also what makes those long-ago memories so golden. I knew every pool, rock, ledge, and deadfall along a mile of Ridley Creek. I fancied I even knew some of the trout on a first-name basis. I knew what hatches were important and when they occurred; I'd designed or discovered flies to match them, and knew just where to go in each season to use them to best effect. I knew the safest crossing points, the mud banks and bramble thickets to avoid and the paths through them, and the spots where wild strawberries hid among bankside shrubbery for a springtime treat. I could confidently fish well into darkness, knowing where the fish were and where the backcast lanes were, and knowing the way out of the water and back to the car as well by touch as by sight.

The latter was equally true about The Pits. Wading was treacherous in the old quarry, steep-sided in some places, with unexpected submerged sandbars and peninsulas in others. Over time I learned them all. Little visible cover meant I had to discover where fish were by fishing the water and noting where I caught things. But once I'd done this, I could go directly from one unmarked hotspot to another. I always fished this lake until well after sunset, enjoying the play of colors washing from the sky reflected in its deep waters, and the coming and going of waterfowl. When only stars were mirrored in the water, and the chugs and snaps of the evening rise had waned, I waded out, never once mis-stepping into the deeper water, clambered up one of my obscure paths up the quarry sides, and biked home amidst flickering fireflies and whirring cicadas.

It didn't matter that these waters were not world-class fisheries. It didn't matter that the fish in The Pits were a bit on the small side, or that the trout in Ridley were nearly all stocked fish. When you know old friends that well, you tend to overlook their faults, and just love them for what they are. I always had the feeling that they were just as forgiving of my angling shortcomings. I belonged; the fish, the waters they lived in, and me: We were all part of the same ecosystem. We shared secrets no casual angler could guess, and delighted in the knowledge.

These days, I have a car. Thousands of square miles of territory are accessible for me to explore. Conversely, I no longer have the time to fish two or three times a week. I spend less time on the water, and spread that time among a number of different streams, lakes, and rivers. There are a few that I know fairly well, fishing them twice a year, sometimes fishing them several days in succession before returning to home and job for another six months. I know certain pools, holes, drop-offs, cuts, and other holding water, and can make a good educated guess at what flies I'll need when I go fish them. But they are just acquaintances, ones I regret not having the time to get to know well enough to call them friends. They welcome me back each time I visit, but we part with no lasting regrets. I fondly talk about them and show photos of them, but it strikes me I never even took pictures of Ridley or The Pits. I didn't need to; it would have been a self-portrait.

There are lots of advantages to this gypsy style of fishing: a wider variety of fish species and water types, opportunities for solitude in remote places, the chance of catching a lunker, or the elusive beauty of wild fish. Some waters are twenty minutes from home, some a five-hour drive; some easy access, others requiring long drives down mazes of back roads or rigorous hiking to reach. If water conditions or other factors turn off the fish on one stream, I have other choices, not to mention finding the variety itself stimulating.

Still I find it ineffably sad that I no longer have a deep relationship with any given piece of water, and keep promising myself that this will change once I retire. Several streams I visit have an ambiance that tells me we could have an intimate friendship. My dream is to buy a retirement home near one of these, and spend my golden years becoming one with my chosen home waters. Some people may think I'm a trifle warped to be looking for the Perfect Stream instead of Mr. Right. These people are obviously not fly fishers.

Spring 2003

The Third Season
By Donna Trexler

I vividly remember my first fly-fishing outing in April 2000. Who could forget a beautiful but cool April day spent mostly trying to extricate a fly from bushes after just about every attempt at casting? Even after a quick dip in the chilly waters of the Little Lehigh I gamely persisted in my attempts to get my fly onto the water. Fortunately for my angling future I discovered that for me, fishing is not merely about the catching, equally important is the watching. Within me I felt the first stirrings of what was to become a deep and abiding love for the trout I could see hanging opportunistically in the crystal waters. There was to be no fish for me that day; indeed, not for a long time thereafter would my inept, but earnest efforts be rewarded.

There were precious few fish of any persuasion caught that first season, but despite my notable lack of success I persevered and was finally rewarded with a fine fat rainbow trout caught that fall on the club trip to Potter County. The catching part is not the only gratification I get from fishing; but, let's face it, everyone needs some positive reinforcement. The feeling of that pulsing piscine life at the end of my line resonated within me in a way I can't begin to explain. I thanked that beauty for granting me a brief intersection with an alien life form and gave it a kiss before releasing it back into its own element to live what I hoped would be a long and productive life. I was in love.

I spent the autumn after that first season learning how to tie my own flies. When you lose as many flies as I did you should either have deep pockets or learn to tie your own. The winter was spent feverishly tying flies in anticipation of spring. No matter that they were as ugly as a dead rat's ass and had a tendency to fall apart, I happily tied away.

The second season began much as the first had. My casting was clumsy and inaccurate. I spent a lot of time retrieving my home-tied and half-nude flies from trees and shrubs. I put down more fish than I care to think about. Still, I fished, sometimes two or three times a week. More importantly, I watched. I watched the hatching of caddis and mayflies. I watched their mating dance as they sought to perpetuate their species. I stood transfixed in the center of a mating swarm and marveled as the small dun-colored caddis laid their bright eggs on my damp waders. Especially entrancing was the graceful aerial ballet of the mayfly spinners. I watched the trout and their manner of feeding during a hatch and at spinner fall. I watched, and learned, and caught, mostly by accident I thought, an occasional fish.

Winter was again spent feverishly tying flies in anticipation of spring. The flies were beginning to look a little better. Except for the fact that my casting had slightly improved, my third season started out pretty much the same as the second. My regular rounds of the local streams resulted in precious few trout. Oh, there was the occasional accidental catch, but things were slow. In May I went to Spruce Creek on one of Ann McIntosh's trips set up through Spruce Creek Outfitters. While the trip was pretty much rained out, I did get to spend half a day on Spruce with Skip Galbraith as my guide. The stream was high and getting muddier by the second, but dragging a big, bright streamer near the bottom did result in one nice fish that was no accident. According to Skip I would have done better to strike more often. The day after the rain I braved the Little Juniata which was high and muddy. I drifted a San Juan Worm around a boulder and a nice little brown took my offering. The catching part was definitely picking up.

I spent most of the summer fishing the Brandywine for panfish. Boy, did I have some spectacular results using Fishy's hopper and Mary's cricket. I felt like I was queen of the Brandywine. In addition to my solo outings my husband, Tim (he who fishes only to accommodate me), and I enjoyed regular Wednesday evening fishing and dinner dates. By late summer I felt ready to try my true loves, the trout, again, so in September I headed back to Spruce Creek with Ann. We had scheduled a guided day on Spruce with Skip, and what a great day it turned out to be. Skip is a very good guide, and if you let him know you want criticism and teaching that is what he will give you. Very early on Skip pointed to a narrow slot between tree branches and told me to place my fly near the shore between those branches. Imagine my surprise when I did exactly what he told me to do. Well, he had created a casting monster. I casted as if no spot was too difficult for me to reach, I casted with the assurance that comes from using an endless supply of home-tied flies; in short, I casted to some pretty difficult places, and I caught fish. And the catching was no accident. There was the sweet moment when casting Mary's cricket into a spot overhung with shrubs resulted in a very large brown being hooked and landed. The next day Ann and I fished the Little Juniata. I caught, and caught more. We found ourselves in the middle of a white fly hatch in the evening. I delighted in choosing what I thought was a fair emerger pattern from my fly box and was even more delighted when I caught a trout. The catching part was definitely improving.

I returned to Potter County for the club trip in the fall. Even though I'd been skunked the previous year, I returned because I enjoyed the camaraderie as well as the scenery. It's good watching territory. This fall turned out to be quite different from the previous. First there were the bears, lots of big bears putting on garbage can fat for the coming hibernation. Of course I am not one to put myself between a bear and its meal, so there were no problematic encounters. Then there were the fish. Nancy and Jake Jacobsen, also in Potter County for the fishing, advised us of a spot where the wild brookies were plentiful. I walked downstream a bit and caught a couple of little beauties. They shone like gems in the sunlight. I spotted what looked to me like a prime lie. The casting was not too difficult, I placed my fly and *bam* the trout took it, but I struck too late and missed. I tried again, but that fish was down so I spent the rest of the day heading upstream catching one beautiful brookie after another. These were small fish of six to eight inches on a very small stream. I felt blessed to have caught them. It was a miracle, and I loved each and every one of them. But, by the end of the day I just had to go back to the trout in the prime lie. I positioned myself just down and across from the lie and placed my cast from a kneeling position. *Bam*, the brookie hit the fly, I struck and this time I had him, the biggest, brightest, most beautiful brookie of the day. This was no accident. The catching was definitely good.

This winter I plan to tie a lot of flies in anticipation of the fourth season which I hope will be as good as the third. However, one of the many things that I have learned in three seasons is that there are no guarantees, so if the fishing isn't good you'll find me watching.

Spring 2003

Spring Ahead!
By Rabbit Jensen

It starts when the male groundhogs, driven from their snug burrows by the mating urge, poke their whiskered snouts out into the cold, snowy air. The day devoted to this creature's emergence is no minor holiday to me. It's the day I also stir from my winter hibernation, feeling the first twinges of Cabin Fever. *I'd better start tying flies*, I think. Soon the mating calls of owls wake me in the cold night, wake me from dreams of rising fish. I snuggle back into my nest of blankets, seeking to recapture those dreams. Then the startling green of wild leeks sprout from snow that looks suddenly soft and tired. I can't resist; I clip the stalks for omelets or creamy potato soup.

The leeks are closely followed by crocus, my favorite flowers because they are the first of the year. They close their blossoms tightly against the chill of night, then spread their petals to the sun, gaudy purple teacups drinking in the warmth, bright against the lingering snow. Just a few warm days during crocus season can bring trout to the surface, chasing emerging Early Black Stoneflies. If not, a tiny Pheasant Tail nymph might interest them, for the mayflies I call "snowflies" are active in some streams even in February. If I can become active enough myself to stand in streamside snow to fish for them.

In the tiny headwater creek that crosses my land, pallid green watercress is at its sweet best. Daffodils send up clumps of green, naturalized throughout my woodlot, then swelling yellow buds burst into a fanfare of golden trumpets. More often than not they are then buried by the winter's heaviest snowfalls. Forsythia blooms wear chill white caps. The calendar says spring, but the Equinox usually signals winter's last defiant tantrum, the March blizzard.

But its fury is quickly spent, and its melting swells the streams into rushing torrents. The snow rapidly fades away, revealing the indigo stars of myrtle blooms bright against their sturdy dark green leaves. The daffodils shake off their snowy burden and stand tall and proud among them. *It's almost Opening Day, better get my tackle ready*, I remind myself.

Winter concedes the match, but has one or two more light snows for us, both a warning that it will return, and a final blessing on the land. My father and I have our traditional friendly argument. "This one's the onion snow," he insists. I gaze unfocused at the sky, and reply, "Nope. One more." With eighty springs of experience behind him, his weather wisdom usually wins, but I don't grudge him the victory. The farmers' plows turn that last snow into the soil, leaving moist dark furrows eager to welcome the seed.

Opening Day passes with a weekend of feverish activity. In my case, not fishing, amidst the crowds and the lingering winter cold; preparing my tackle for my personal season's debut, a week or two later.

Up in the mountains, along the verges of muddy dirt roads, coltsfoot nods its shaggy blonde head. My pickup truck splashes through coffee-colored puddles, adding fresh brown freckles to the previous day's layer of dried tan mud. It's late morning. No point in fishing the frigid early hours; the fish will not stir from their winter torpor until the sun has warmed the water. I slept until nine, then enjoyed a leisurely hot breakfast—civilized fishing, my favorite of the year. On the stream, opportunistic wild trout occasionally slash at the ubiquitous caddis, but the caddis are just the warm-up act. The star attraction is the Blue Quill Mayfly, which comes onstage at two o'clock, plays a brief but glorious set, then exits to my enthusiastic applause. For forty minutes, beautiful midnight-blue mayflies swarm upwards, and beautiful wild browns and native brookies take them, and my imitation, with gusto. The hatch ends as suddenly as it began, the sated fish sinking contentedly back into cover. I linger awhile, watching a single tardy Blue Quill perched on my sleeve, stretching its drying wings, exquisitely delicate. I breathe air rich with the scent of life renewing itself, spiced with the aroma of trout on my hands. *After all that waiting and preparation*, I think gratefully. *Spring is finally here!*

Spring 2004

A Much Needed Vacation
By Judy Wilson

I have never needed a vacation as badly as I had needed this one. I decided to go fly fishing for five or six days. I contemplated for days where to go and what to do. With advice from lots of people, including Mary and Rabbit, I decided on the Yellow Breeches. It was far enough away from home, but also close enough that I wasn't driving for hours. Fly fishing always cleans the cobwebs out of my brain and settles me like nothing else in the world.

I arrived in Boiling Springs on August 21st. There was a huge rainstorm while I was driving there. I went to the Yellow Breeches Fly Shop and asked some questions. Everything was muddy and there was no fishing to be had for a couple of days. I asked about Mountain Creek in Pine Grove Furnace State Park. The guy behind the counter was surprised I knew about that creek. I had researched trout streams in proximity to the Yellow Breeches in Dwight Landis' book, *Trout Streams of Pennsylvania*. I also remembered the park from a camping trip in college. I remembered its beauty, shade and tall pine trees.

It took me about an hour to drive there and I got there about 8:30 in the morning. I saw this beautiful cold creek rushing past. It was crystal clear and there were no people around. I hiked a ways down the path and waded in. I tied on a small ant and *bang*; before I could react, something hit the fly and was gone. I tried another cast and the same thing happened. I looked at the fly and it was about a 14. I had an 18 so I tied that on instead. This time I cast the fly, the fish hit it and I brought in one of the most beautiful fish I had ever seen. It was a wild brook trout. It was about 4 inches long, had a red stripe down each side, and was very feisty. I fished the rest of the morning along this beautiful stream and caught about ten of these beautiful little fish. When I finally looked at my watch, it was 2 p.m. I had lunch among tall pines at an aged picnic table and felt like a new woman.

There are two lakes in this state park and it is usually crowded on the weekend. As this was a Sunday, it was becoming more and more crowded. I wandered farther down the trail about a mile and waded in again. The fishing was fabulous. I caught and released fish all the rest of the afternoon. The biggest one was about 6 inches long. They are small but feisty.

The next day, I went out to the Yellow Breeches. I went to Allenberry and parked in the "Fishermen's Lot." I fished for a few hours and caught a few small brown trout, but felt like something was wrong. I stopped for lunch and went to the fly shop again. They suggested smaller flies. I tried that and it was somewhat better, but I did not feel like I knew what I was doing. The water was high and fast and I was uncomfortable. I had torn some ligaments in my ankle last winter and I was feeling it. I fished the rest of the day and stayed for the white fly hatch. I caught a couple of trout, but felt like something was missing.

The next day, August 23rd, I went to "the run" of the Yellow Breeches. This is the place where the lake empties into a stream under a blanket of trees. I was fishing with nymphs and not catching much. One of the older guys on the stream asked to see my flies. I was using a #16 Gold-Ribbed Hare's Ear. He said, "Try one of these," and handed me a bead-head Zebra Midge in a size 22. He gave me two and I thanked him, tied one on and had the first of many brown trout. My flies were all too big. I went to the fly shop after lunch and bought a bunch of flies in smaller sizes. That was the missing link. Once I had the right size fly, I caught all the fish that I wanted. There are lots of different kinds of trout on the Yellow Breeches. There are brown trout, rainbow trout, brook trout and even palomino trout. I have caught lots of trout before, but not like these. These were truly the most beautiful fish I had ever seen. Their colors were spectacular.

I fished this area of the run down to the stream behind Allenberry for the remainder of my time at the Yellow Breeches. It was fun and I felt totally restored by fly fishing. It is amazing what a few days off fishing by yourself can do for a person.

There were lots of people there fishing. They were all incredibly friendly and helpful. I met a woman there who remarked that she never sees other women fly fishing. We spent the rest of the day together. She has read about our group on the Internet and I encouraged her to join. I have learned so much from being a part of DVWFFA.

On the day I left, there was this man who had been fishing for hours and not catching anything. He said he was disgusted, watching me pull in fish after fish. I asked him what kinds of flies he was using. He showed me some nymphs in size 12 and 14. I gave him a couple of bead-head Zebra nymphs, in size 22, just like someone had given me. What goes around comes around.

I love fly fishing. It is one part of my very full life that doesn't consume me.

Autumn 2004

Susan Proulx takes a fine autumn brown trout.

Cycles
By Rabbit Jensen

It's spring and everything is new! Well, "new" and yet comfortably familiar. Brilliant green sprouts appear in the garden, newborn progeny of last year's bulbs. On pin oak trees, this year's buds swell eagerly, pushing last year's dried brown leaves from their death-grip. Both have a destiny to fulfill: the new to grow, the old to decay, both to nurture the tree that bore them. The silence of winter ends decisively as birds begin their mating songs, just as their parents did a year earlier, the same songs in new voices. The sun rises a little earlier each day, warming waters chill and high with snowmelt. In response, nymphs become restless, instinct prodding them away from their comfortable life to their next great adventure. As if by plan, fish stir from their winter torpor and find themselves hungry.

So do the bears, stirring from their cozy dens. And so do I, stirring from mine. But my hunger is spiritual. No matter the storms that battered my soul over the winter, no matter if I had been buried deep in troubles like heavy snow, spring renews me; ever-new but ever-familiar. The weight of the fishing vest, the cold clamp of water pressing my waders against my legs, and the subconscious relaxation exercise before the first cast: I take several deep, slow breaths of clean fresh air scented with mud, evergreens, growing things, and the elusive aroma of running water. Relaxation starts with my scalp and sinks down, until I can feel the running water washing my stress away. Time slows, like a guitar string loosening, until its pitch approaches and finally matches the tone and rhythm of the natural world.

At that moment I comprehend with every particle of my being that I am a part of the natural world—and its never-ending cycles. And every particle of my being will partake in the circle of life-death-life, just as every other living thing does. More than that: Since Nature recycles every particle of matter, how can the soul be an exception? The first fishing trip in spring restores my sense of the Eternal, as it happens all around me, and in me. The loss of loved ones in the year past loses its sting. They are all around me, in the mayfly mating minuet whose joyous beauty has a single purpose: the future generation. In the Royal Coachman which works as well for me as it did for my father, and his forebears. In the grand cycle of rushing water, small streams meeting and mating to become mighty rivers, finally all sinking into the serenity of the sea; from there, to rise, a molecule at a time, to form clouds that rain down on the mountains, creating small streams once again; purified and renewed in the process, just as I will be between this cycle and the next.

For some of us, fly fishing is, and ever will be, more than a mere sport or hobby. Obsession? Meditation in motion? Possibly even religion? Outsiders will never understand, but *we* know why.

Spring 2006

Can One Fish Change Your Life?
By Cheri Poole

Although I arrived in Cancun a day late due to the March ice storm, I knew from my many years of traveling to Boca Paila, someone from the lodge would be there to meet me and take me to one of my favorite fishing destinations. After the two-hour drive down the familiar road, I was greeted by Chico, the lodge manager and went to find Francisco, my favorite bartender, who would make me a Margarita: the type you can only get in Boca.

My husband, Jerry, went a day earlier and as we parted in the Philly airport, I assured him we would meet for dinner on Monday evening to celebrate his first Grand Slam of the week; and he didn't disappoint me. After a wonderful meal, we fell asleep to the sound of ocean waves and the wind blowing the palm trees outside the window. I am sure you can tell, I truly love this place, but back to my fish story...

We went to the dock early on Tuesday to meet Alfonso, who is a fantastic guide with most likely the best eyes in the place. I was quite nervous as I did not want to disappoint him. I was certain after Jerry's Slam the day before, he might see me and think, "Oh great, here comes the wife and she wants to fish." I did feel confident that I had prepared, that I had done this before, and most importantly, that I was not going to let what anyone else (including my husband) thought, bother me. We generally take turns on the front of the boat and today I went first. I hooked a bonefish right away using a crab fly. Hearing the reel sing as the fish took off relieved some of my "first day out" anxiety and I started to relax.

Shortly after landing the bonefish, Alfonso's tone changed and got a bit rushed as he said, "Permit coming. Ten o'clock... cast now... more left... *shoot it!*" As anyone who has fished saltwater knows, there is nothing more exciting than a permit within casting range and nothing more unnerving. Permit have a magical ability to turn your cast into something unrecognizable, your line into a large knotted mess in the bottom of the boat, and generally wreak havoc with your entire nervous system. I did, however, manage to make a decent cast about forty feet out, wait, and start stripping in; long, slow, and then faster strips. Just as I felt the unmistakable tug, Alfonso said, "Set it!" I did and off the fish went!

He ran far out, very fast and I would only allow myself to think ever so slightly that there was a P-E-R-M-I-T on the end of my line. I kept repeating to myself, "It's only a fish… it's only a fish…" After several runs and a gentle coaxing in, *I got it in the boat!* I won't repeat exactly what I said, but I am shaking now as I write, because this was my first permit on a fly. Jerry caught his first one last May in Honduras, both of us trying unsuccessfully for eight years. He tried to explain to me the feeling that washes over you when your first permit lands in the boat; a life-changing feeling. I now understand. Something absolutely washed over me that morning. It wasn't that the fish was big (he was only about 3 pounds), it was because he was a permit and I caught him on a fly!

Our day went on to be completely amazing, as Jerry soon after boated a bonefish, a ten pound permit and a snook. After lunch, we went deep back into the mangroves and both caught small tarpon to complete my first-ever Grand Slam and Jerry's first-ever Super Grand Slam. Even better that we did it in the same boat on the same day! Life just wasn't going to get any better.

The next day started out very much like the previous one. We headed far to the south, to the same flat where we picked up the permits and bones the day before. Jerry caught his bonefish right away and I took over the front of the boat.

Suddenly, Alfonso's tone changed and the energy in the boat was electrified. "Permit… big one… eleven o'clock… a hundred feet, coming closer… go now, fifty feet… it's castable."

I thought, "Oh, great. I had a good day yesterday and now he expects more (note the extra ten feet)." However, in the same instant I thought, "I did this yesterday—I can and will give it my best shot." I made several casts, finally placed the fly to the fish's liking and *he took it!* He sped off well into my backing while I anchored the butt of the rod into my stomach and decided I had just better hold on. After fighting for about fifteen minutes, in what was very much a battle of wills, I landed a fourteen pound permit. After the photos were taken and the fish released, it took a good half an hour for me to quit shaking. Jerry landed an eighteen-pounder later that morning and before the day was over, he had another

Super Slam and I, another Grand Slam. Clearly the "Fish Gods" were smiling on us.

Catching not one, but two permit and Slamming with my husband in the same boat, two days in a row, has quite a Wow Factor, but it all started with the first little three-pounder. Often times now when my "new self" arises in our daily lives, my husband mutters to himself, "Damn fish," but always with a wink and a grin. It could be years before I catch another, but nothing can take away the feeling of completing an achievement that was much more than I imagined. Life after permit is good.

Summer 2007

The Farewell Brookie
By Rabbit Jensen

The last day of the annual fall trip to Potter County I'm too busy to be sad. The cabin has to be cleaned out and cleaned up by check-out time, so I'm up early. By the time my pick-up truck is packed, I'm tired already, and still have to face a four-hour drive home and unpacking the truck when I get there. Therefore, although it's still morning when I leave, I seldom stop and fish on the way. But for some reason, this year as I drove up Rt. 44, my mind was still filled with visions of colorful brook trout flashing and swirling. With each one I'd caught through the week, I'd felt that elusive, vital connection between myself and the wild energy of these gorgeous spawners. It was heartbreaking to leave them behind without even a chance to say farewell. The temptation was irresistible. Putting the truck in 4WD, I headed for the headwaters of Kettle Creek.

As I donned my gear, I felt refreshingly adventurous and free, with a touch of wild energy of my own. It had been a long time since I'd fished without a companion, or at least telling someone where I'd be. I strolled along the trail back to a favorite run, all my senses engaged in enjoying the autumn forest. The leaves, the sky overhead, the tracks limned in the mud, all were stored in my memory for solace in the bleak winter to come.

The run had changed in the summer floods, the far bank becoming even more undercut; saplings sporting leaves of gold or pink that once stood tall on the opposite bank, now leaned over the stream at angles, providing excellent cover for the fish—and making casting hell for the angler. One nice hole I reached only by drifting my Yellow Humpy down under the branches, where a fish slashed at it. A poor hooking angle, I thought as I disentangled my fly from the results of my futile strike.

Farther up the run, I dropped my fly along a drop-off, and hooked a trout solidly. Strong and wily, this fellow tried to dive into some downed branches, but finally came to hand: a wild brown about a foot long, stunningly marked with big red and black spots. He had the well-defined facial features and big dark eyes the old-timers indentify with "Loch Levin browns." I was pleased to land this, my second brown of the trip, and shook him off the hook underwater with a sincere compliment and wish for his future welfare.

At the head of the run, a fallen log at an angle to a fast current has dug a hole at its tip, and a lucky cast swept my fly along the log and into that hole, where a fine male brookie savaged it. I played this fish just close enough to identify him clearly, when an acrobatic twist freed him from my hook and he shot back into the depths. Once more I had colorful autumn brook trout in my mind, the reality matching the memories, so I couldn't help but smile.

From here I crossed at the riffle, setting up for the next pool upstream. On my side, the shallow side, a thick mat of golden leaves had been deposited in the slow water. I stopped at its edge, not wanting to disturb the process of solar energy turning to trout: the leaves nurtured by the sun, now sheltering and feeding myriad nymphs which in turn would nurture fish. But even while the leaves invoked the season past, and the nymphs thoughts of the future, I was focused in the present. Between the leaf mat and the huge leaning sycamore that defines this pool, the water is very deep, and contains plenty of trout, all as canny as only wild fish in still water can be. I crept, step by step, cast by cast, as slow and quiet as I know how, until at last I could lay a long, delicate cast right into the current sweeping past the sycamore's trunk. It bobbed down the current, out of the hot spot—I thought. The take came as a surprise, and I felt only a moment's resistance before the fly came back at me.

Clouds had covered the sun, and I feared a return of the rain that had plagued us on and off the last three days. I decided I had one more chance at my farewell brookie: an old friend that lurked downstream of the bridge abutment near where I'd parked my truck. In past trips, two friends had caught him, and I'd done so myself, on a Yellow Humpy identical to the one on my tippet. Crossing the riffle again, I hiked across the floodplain meadow, dotted with the pink pompoms of English clover, brightened by clumps of purple aster and blazing yellow goldenrod. I paused under a crab-apple tree, its boughs heavy with clusters of fruit. There were no windfalls underneath; it seems the local deer, turkeys, and grouse have a taste for these tart morsels. I strolled on, retracing my steps along the trail, in no hurry despite the threat of rain. This would be my last walk in the Potter County woods this year, and I wanted to savor the sights, sounds, and aromas.

In the middle of the mud-caked plank bridge I stopped to lean on the rusty railing and peer downstream. Three almost-identical sections of a lightning-blasted tree trunk had lodged in the shallow run below, at casually-precise angles and spacing that reminded me of objets d'arte scattered across a Dali landscape. Directly below me, the bridge abutment took a sharp corner to meet the bank, but the current bubbling along it continued straight until the bank curved out to meet it downstream. The triangle of deep, still water between abutment, bank, and current was the lair of my friend Mr. Big Brookie.

Clouds continued to darken overhead, and I knew my time in Potter County was rapidly coming to an end. Crossing the bridge, I walked downstream looking for an easy path down the steep bank, waded in and took position to cast to my old adversary. I worked line out, concentrating on that tranquil corner the trout called home, gauging the length of my cast and the currents between us, going for the perfect presentation.

At last, the fly landed where I wanted it and rode jauntily over the big fellow's lie. A tiny dimple sucked the fly under. I'd been expecting an attractor-style rise, not a timid terrestrial sip. By the time I struck, there was nothing there. The old patriarch had fooled me neatly, and I acknowledged it with a low laugh.

He had all the time he needed to recover from our encounter, but the smell of rain on the breeze told me my time in this place was over. I waded out, but before I stepped onto the bank, I looked back at the brookie's lie, brought my fly rod to the salute, and intoned, *Ave Salvelinius!* I hadn't caught my farewell brookie, but we'd exchanged our good-byes.

Winter 2007

My First Trout on a Fly
By Mary S. Kuss

It's funny how memory works. We tend to assume our memory records everything with perfect accuracy, like a tape recorder or video camera, for us to play back whenever we want or need to. But of course that's not true. No two people will recall a shared experience in exactly the same way. Memory is clearly a subjective thing, more fluid and mutable than we'd like to believe. That fact, however, is a blessing as often as it's a curse.

Having arrived at a point in my life where I most likely have more fly fishing days behind me than ahead, I find myself indulging more and more in pleasant reveries of earlier times. This is especially true during the winter, when conditions do not favor getting out fishing. As I write this in mid-February, I feel very fortunate to have a bountiful trove of delightful memories, inaccurate as they may be, to call upon for my amusement.

It's quite curious what I remember and what I don't. I don't remember the first fish I ever caught, but I do remember the first one that got away. I remember the first smallmouth bass I caught, but I don't recall if it was also my first bass ever or if a largemouth or two preceded it. I don't remember the first trout I caught, but I do remember my first wild trout. And I do remember quite clearly, or so it seems to me, the first trout I ever caught on a fly.

I was born and raised in Point Pleasant, New Jersey. Although a river doesn't exactly run *through* Point Pleasant, it is bordered by the Beaver Dam Creek and the Manasquan River. I spent my youth fishing and crabbing and swimming in the Manasquan. In fact, I was born along its very banks in the former Point Pleasant Hospital. A short river by most standards, you can easily drive from its headwaters in Monmouth County to the Manasquan Inlet, where it flows straight into the Atlantic Ocean, in well under one hour. Its upper reaches are stocked with trout by the state, right down to the tidal boundary. It's not surprising that some of these trout drop down into the estuary to feast on grass shrimp, killifish, juvenile blue crabs, and the myriad of other forage available there. Or that these well-fed fish, many having put on substantial size and weight, eventually swim back upstream again.

The Manasquan bears very little resemblance to a classic trout stream. The banks are steep and composed of highly erodible, loamy clay. For that reason, the water is never really clear. It's rare to be able to see to the bottom in more than a foot of water. This lack of visibility, combined with high banks, make wade fishing dangerous and difficult if not quite impossible. I don't recall ever seeing anyone attempt it. The Manasquan is obviously not fly fishing friendly, and not much of a trout stream. Still, it's what I had to work with. And having pulled numerous trout from its waters on spinning tackle and bait I now wanted badly to catch one on a fly.

I was not yet keeping an angling log, but I would guess it must have been 1969. We had endured a long dry period that summer. The water was low and as clear as I'd ever seen it. Large tracts of forested land in New Jersey were being totally defoliated by a heavy infestation of Gypsy Moths. The emergence of the adult moths coincided perfectly with the unusually low, clear water in the Manasquan. The stage was set for some very interesting fishing.

Joe Spader, one of my fly fishing mentors, had alerted me to what was happening and suggested I try fishing the Brice Park area. When I arrived that late afternoon Joe was already there, and had just landed a beautiful hook-jawed male brown trout of nearly 20 inches on a big deer hair salmon fly that was a good match for the moths in size and color. This was before catch and release philosophy had really caught on, and Joe had killed the fish and hung it from a low tree branch. He later told me that when he cleaned and cooked that trout its flesh was as orange as a salmon's and just as delicious. The fish had clearly been down into the estuary, if not actually to sea.

I didn't catch any fish that day, but I was highly motivated to return the very next day. I walked to the area where Joe had caught his big trout, and wandered downstream to try to find a fish for myself. Moths were falling into the water in numbers, fluttering on the surface. It wasn't long before I saw a moth disappear into an impressive rise where the current ran tight against a stump along the far bank. There was no room for a backcast. Although the stream banks were closely lined with trees and shrubs I was able to find an opening opposite the fish's lie that would allow a roll cast. Today I could make that cast easily. Then, however, my skill level and my equipment conspired to make it a formidable challenge.

I didn't have a lot of flies to choose from, but I found one dry fly with brown hackle that was as close as I could come to a match for the moths. I knotted it to my leader, and began roll casting toward my target. Attempt after attempt fell short, but at least I had not put the fish down. She continued to rise, taking several more moths. Finally in desperation I threw the most prodigious roll cast I could, all force and no control. The fly overshot the mark and landed far back in the eddy above the stump. "Oh no!" I groaned. Quickly the slack played out of the leader and the fly began to drag.

There was nothing I could do but watch it dribble along the edge of the stump, sure that the fish would be put down by such a horrible performance. Then it happened. A flash of silver, and the fly disappeared! My heart raced as the fish put a deep bend in my rod. In my excitement and inexperience I'm sure I made plenty of mistakes, yet somehow the trout stayed on the hook. I had no landing net, and could not have reached the water with one anyway. There was no recourse, I had to lift the fish up and swing her onto the bank. Had my trout been as big as Joe's, I would surely have lost her. But in a brief anxious moment the fat, 13-inch rainbow henfish lay flopping on the ground at my feet. A quick pounce and she was mine, to my utter delight.

How factually accurate is this account? Who can say? Yet the vivid images remain with me to this day: Joe's big brown hanging from the branch, the golden gravel of the stream bed, the fluttering brown moths, my fly skirting the edge of the stump and disappearing into that rise. These memories and many others like them are my treasures, the bright and enduring legacy of the years I've spent fishing.

Spring 2008

Silver and Gold
By Rabbit Jensen

Gold are the birch leaves crunching under my boots,
Under a canopy of gold upheld by trunks of silver.
Weeds by the amber-colored river sparkle gemlike with frost.
I wade cautiously into the frigid rushing water,
Its mysterious depths unplumbed by the October sunrise.
Its darkness is a perfect mirror for the sugar maples.
Their leaves reflect ripples of gold, between banks of golden trees.
Then an arch of silver vaults from the water,
Breaking the golden patterns in a sudden gleam of metallic life.
I contemplate my fly, a match for the autumn colors,
Fiery orange, tawny bronze, flashing gold and silver.
Perhaps it blends in too well, for the salmon snub it.
They fling their silvery bodies into the sunlight,
Perhaps to tease me; or perhaps aware
Only of their own beauty, and their joy in life.
I share their joy. The only wealth I treasure
Is to be a part of their molten golden river,
To be a minor gem set in their world of precious metal.

Winter 2004

Stripers By Day, Lobsters By Night, Fishing Friendships
By Nancy Keyak Simpson

Rain, thick fog, bright sunshine, humidity, coolness, lighthouses, history, fine dining, belted cows, lobsters, bird-watching, seals, celebrity-watching... oh and "ayuh," fishing. What happens along the Kennebec and St. George Rivers of Maine, as the full moon raises the waters to higher levels?

Maine has always been one of my favorite states. As much as Neal and I have visited Maine, this was the first time I was in Maine to fly fish for stripers. Our superb host Bonnie had given us a special opportunity to walk the life of a local, to roam the rivers with the lobstermen and fishing community, to observe nature "off the beaten track," to partake in some history, relax with smart, funny and talented fishing friends, and to enjoy fabulous food. As a lobster lover, I found it truly incredible indulging in lobster that was freshly pulled from the traps and brought back home to cook within a half hour's time.

We arose very, very early in the morning on our fishing days, to find ourselves thick in mist and fog and wondering where along the rivers we were. Peacefulness overtakes you as you sip your coffee, peer through the mist, listen for splashes, casting here and there. The river knowledge of our fishing guides was quite impressive—even as the fog was thick enough to challenge the sense of direction for even one of the more experienced locals. As the mist lifted, the scenery and river life expanded (and the layers of clothing lessened!). I was getting a more intimate view of a river that I had previously only seen while driving along the highways and bridges getting to somewhere else.

We watched a lobsterman show us the gadgetry that helped him lift his lobster traps. He held up and measured a lobster that was the perfect 1¾ pounder that I would normally order! The lobster and fishing life is clearly challenging and they all look out for each other on these waters.

While meandering along the rivers in pursuit of the elusive stripers, we passed where Kevin Costner stayed and fly fished with his sons while filming a movie (apparently he is quite a good fly fisherman). Late one day, we spied an esteemed Wyeth grandson who snuck in from his island and artistic endeavors to casually dine alongside of us at a picnic table on a dock. Jamie's sighting reminded us of our visit to the Olsen house right down the road from Bonnie in Cushing and the richness of the artistic community surrounding us.

These rivers are the homes of the Great Blue Heron, Ospreys, Bald Eagles, numerous *fish* of course, and many fabulous sea critters. I was intrigued by the seal whose big round eyes kept peering at me above the water several times while on the Kennebec—splashing loudly as he dove underwater and reappeared elsewhere. His curiosity was triggered by my casting and the hopes that I would hook a fish that would become this seal's dinner should he steal it from me! I'll never look at those cute seals the same again!

Our folks caught a striper, pollock, and all-in-all enjoyed time to unwind, try our hand at striper casting, dine very well, and certainly cherish the scenery and friendships that make us glad to be a part of the DVWFFA.

Fall 2008

In The Beginning...
By Mary S. Kuss

How did I begin my journey as a flyfisher and tier? It all happened so long ago, the precise details have dimmed with the passage of years. Even so some bright spots of memory remain, like dappled sunshine on a shady streamside trail.

Before fly fishing, there was just plain fishing. At age six, my first rod was a slender limb cut from a weedy tree by my Uncle Marvin and tipped with an equal length of braided black nylon line stolen from his baitcast reel. There was a round red-and-white bobber, a split shot, a #10 Eagle Claw hook and a Prince Albert can full of garden worms. Next came a bamboo pole, then a baitcast outfit of my own with a reel that gave me plenty of backlashes to pick out. This developed a lot of character, and also the patience that would later be such an asset to me in fishing and in life in general. I moved on to a spinning rod, and finally a fly rod.

That first fly rod was a Shakespeare "Wonder Rod," an 8-foot 8-weight fiberglass stick, heavy and floppy and perfectly awful in comparison to today's fly rods. But it was mine and I loved it. A maroon-painted South Bend Finalist reel spooled with a garish "torpedo taper" line completed my rig. The entire kit was courtesy of my Mother's S&H Green Stamps.

My first "flies" were very cheap cork poppers imported from somewhere in the Far East. These were sold as an assortment, packed in a little round plastic container divided into wedge-shaped compartments like a pie. Although the poppers came in various colors, the yellow one seemed to work the best and was my favorite. My family was quite poor, and lack of funding was a recurring theme in my early fishing. Replacement poppers were not always immediately available, so my supply was used with great care.

As a fly fishing instructor, I know that the most common casting error made by novices is to break the wrist on the backcast, thus throwing the line and the fly toward the ground behind them. Much as I might like to believe that I was somehow immune to this problem, the events that are recounted below make it clear that I was not.

I was fifteen years old, and in my first summer with the fly rod. My favorite place to fish was "the Gravel Pit Pond." If it had another name, I never found out about it. I would get my Mother or Grandfather to drop me off there and return to pick me up a few hours later. The dirt road that led back to the pond and the gravel pit beyond is gone now, and I suspect the pond is, too. Back then, however, it was in its prime of life—full of bluegill and crappie, bullfrogs and water snakes, and an occasional largemouth bass. The Pond was accessible only from the road side, the far side backed up to a thick swamp. The road itself provided ample backcast room.

One afternoon at the pond I was fishing away and getting enough action to keep me quite happy. I had been making easy short casts and doing well, but gradually the hits got fewer and fewer. Along the far bank what I was sure were larger fish dimpled and swirled seductively. I just *had* to try to reach them. I was whipping away for all I was worth, and almost reaching my target. Then I noticed that my popper no longer seemed to be floating. How could that be? I stripped in my line to inspect the fly. Oh, no! The popper's body was completely gone. In my attempts to cast farther than usual, I had apparently beaten the fly on the ground behind me until the cork disintegrated. All that remained was the hook and a few yellow hackles streaming out behind.

This was an especially disheartening development. The fly box was empty and there was no backup. And Mom would not return to pick me up for another hour and a half. Dejectedly I rolled what was left of my fly out onto the water in front of me and started twitching it along just below the surface. I was quite mesmerized by the action of the hackles in the water. Just as I was thinking how neat this was a larger-than-normal crappie loomed up under the hook and inhaled it. Needless to say, I continued to fish.

It soon became obvious that I was catching more and bigger fish with the accidental wet fly than I previously had with intact poppers! Thus began the search for a nice, bright yellow underwater fly. This was at the very beginning of the "Fly Fishing Renaissance" in the late 1960's. Fly fishing gear was hard to come by, especially near my New Jersey home town where most anglers concentrated on conventional saltwater fishing. A couple of nearby bait and tackle stores had a very modest selection of trout flies, however, and I found a source of Yellow Sally wet flies. These went for forty cents each, which seemed pretty darn expensive. I don't think that my allowance at the time was even a dollar a week, so it was awfully hard to keep myself in flies. That's when I decided I'd have to start tying my own.

I knew nothing about tying flies, and had no source of instruction. So I set out on my own, quite resourcefully if I say so myself. For hooks, I used the same offset Eagle Claws I used for my bait fishing, complete with slices in the shank to hold the worm in place. I had no idea that these were not appropriate for fly tying. I bought a package of dyed yellow saddle hackles, which I cut into pieces to use as both wings and hackle. I got a spool of yellow floss for the bodies, and some fine gold tinsel for ribbing. I didn't buy tying thread. After all, my Mother had plenty of sewing thread that I could use. I couldn't afford a real fly tying vise, so I got a tiny toy machinist's vise at the Woolworth's Five and Dime. I don't remember how I solved the problem of finishing off the head of the fly; apparently I came up with something that worked.

I regret that I don't have any of those earliest flies. I do remember them, however, and they were incredibly bad by any reasonable standard. Even so they caught fish, which was the most important thing. Soon my fly fishing mentors, no doubt impressed with my persistence, took pity on me and helped me to acquire better tools and materials and some reference books.

These were my first steps in a pastime that's kept me happily occupied ever since. And although there have been many other bright spots along the way, sometimes the oldest memories are the best.

Winter 2008

Fragile Miracle
By Rabbit Jensen

Just on impulse, I turned left in Germania to avoid road construction, and found myself driving out of the village southwards. A large yellow sign appeared: **"Pavement Ends."** As always, this gave me a thrill. I'm not enough of an unreconstructed romantic to believe this means I'm entering an eighteenth-century wilderness populated with Seneca Indians paddling birch-bark canoes, but I always feel freer, more self-sufficient, when I see such a literal sign that I'm leaving modern life behind. Secretly, I feel my synthetic clothing is out of place, and I should be wearing buckskin.

On this particularly Monday in May, it was chilly enough that, even in the car, I had a flannel shirt over my customary t-shirt. A stiff breeze tossed the trees, and riffled the surface of a beaver pond I was passing. I slowed to look, spotting the distinctive silhouette of a little blue heron cupping its crooked wings to land. But my subconscious had a destination in mind. It was not fishing weather, not with this wind heralding an approaching cold front, but my subconscious did not know this. *Fish*, it demanded.

Several promising stretches of the Germania Branch beckoned, but my soul yearned for the familiar beauty of my favorite spot on the upper Kettle. I pulled off just before the rickety wooden bridge and geared up. As I hiked down the dirt road to Jake's Pool, my last trip here, almost a year ago, dominated my mind: a single trout, small, thin, and parr-marked, from the "king" lie of this once-incredible pool. This shocking experience had goaded me into more active environmentalism, alerting me to how fragile my beloved Pennsylvania Wilds were. I surveyed the pool with a mixture of apprehension and appreciation. The water flowed deep, wide, and clear; flowers dotted the grassy meadow with color; birds sang, and a distant rumble marked a drumming grouse. But were there trout?

My favorite fly, the X-Caddis, dropped lightly on the water again and again, probing a current seam, floating along the sheer bank, briefly circling in the eddy behind a rock. Halfway up the pool, a hit! Was it a trout, or one of the chubs that had taken over trout lies in other parts of the Kettle last year? I'd never know. I approached that "king" lie, a downed tree diagonal to the current. I missed another hit right off its downstream point, then another a foot or so up the log. Finally the wind died momentarily and I dropped the fly so it drifted into the center of the log's face, and I hooked a trout. No yearling this time, this one was a good seven or eight inches of colorful, healthy wild brook trout. As I released her, I felt cautiously optimistic that the other hits I'd gotten had been siblings of hers.

I fished the next pool up without incident; unless one counts dropping my flex-light in knee-deep water and getting soaked retrieving it. I fished the rest of the afternoon shivering as the wind cooled my sopping flannel shirt, but not caring in the least. By-passing a section of creek littered with blow-downs and edged with brambles, I waded in again at K-Kamp. There I saw the only indication of other human beings since the day-old tire tracks in the private road when I hiked in: A friendly Labrador from a camp across stream was puttering around in the shallow tail of the pool, giving me a wet, doggy grin. Droplets flew from his wagging tail, but he was content to let me go my own way while he went about his own recreation.

I worked cautiously upstream. Despite the headwind, I managed to get a few casts to go where I wanted them, without disturbing this wide, still pool. I knew there were some fairly deep pockets in what looked like uniformly shallow, uninteresting water. The farther upstream, the faster the water, as the bottom grew rockier and the flow was constricted by a grassy islet. I was amused for awhile by a flicker commuting between this islet and the left bank, for some reason known only to him. Was he taking the Lime Sally Stoneflies that I was seeing from time to time or the sparse Mayflies and Caddis that were also hatching?

Fish were taking them. I suddenly realized that, amidst the riffles of that wide current, there were trout noses poking out, greedily gulping the insects riding the surface. Which insects? Bless wild brook trout, they are seldom selective, and the X-Caddis is usually magic for them. It certainly was this time. I worked up that run getting one hit after another, missing most of them. The ones I hooked were mostly yearlings and two-year-olds, bright and feisty, with a salting of larger trout to give me an unexpected tussle. Each one I looked upon as a miracle, confirmation of

Nature's marvelous ability to heal her own injuries, to bounce back from bad years and mankind's abuse. Each one I released with my blessing: to go forth, prosper, and multiply.

I approached the lair of my old friend Mr. Big Brookie with reverence. Certainly nothing could have harmed him in his deep, cold den. Other trout were rising upstream under the bridge, but I dismissed them, stalking the big one carefully, the wind requiring a closer approach than I liked. The cast had to be right in the current running a couple of inches from the bridge abutment, drifting drag-free above him, to tempt this wise old trout. With caution, timing, and luck, I did everything right, and he rose with a splash. Some minutes later I cradled my old friend for release: still not much longer than a foot, but fatter than ever, with colors that no artist will ever find on a palette.

How can one top that? I couldn't. I climbed out and headed back to my car, which was within sight of the bridge. On the way, I picked up the only litter I'd seen all day, a glass bottle at the edge of the parking area. Away from the protection of the stream banks, I felt the full chill of the wind. I stripped off my waders, got in my car and cranked up the heater.

Upstream, Leetonia Road along the Kettle's headwaters was churned to a muddy mess by gas drillers' vehicles, and I dodged construction trucks, backhoes, and tank trucks of the ominous fracking fluid. The road verges were decorated with surveyor's flags and signs. The litter so conspicuously absent downstream was all too prevalent here. Dirt-smeared men in yellow hard-hats gazed at me as I drove past, obviously from a different world than theirs. Here the water was discolored, and the faded "Wild Brook Trout Heritage Waters" signs were an ironic reminder of just how fragile Nature and her miracles really are. After experiencing those miracles directly that day, I knew that, however hopeless the fight may seem, I will continue doing whatever I can to preserve Nature, to give her room to work those miracles. After all, in over a half-century of searching, I've never found a purpose for life more compelling than dry fly fishing for wild brook trout.

Summer 2010

Weird Events
By Mary S. Kuss

Although it's not common, some mighty strange things can happen while fly fishing. It stands to reason that the more hours you spend fishing, the bigger your collection of odd stories will be. Although I don't get to fish nearly as much as I used to, there was a time when I spent an average of probably 200+ days a year fishing at least a little. That quantity of stream time provided plenty of opportunity to amass some stories that sound like whoppers but, hand-to-God, everything related below is factual and without exaggeration. I can't really rate these first two stories on which is higher on the weird scale. They both seem equally surreal. You decide.

Once, while fishing dry flies on Ridley Creek, I lassoed a trout. This was certainly not intentional on my part, and I'm sure it wasn't intentional on the trout's part. Even so, the fish essentially did it to himself. I must have had a lot of slack in my tippet when he offered at my floating fly. I reacted instinctively to the splashy rise, and live weight on the line indicated an apparent hook-up. As I played the fish I saw that he was coming in tail-first. "Oh, no," I thought. "He's foul-hooked." But in fact the trout was not hooked at all. Somehow the fly and tippet were pulled underwater in such a way that the fly looped around and the standing part of the leader got inside the hook bend, effectively forming a slip knot that then tightened around the wrist of the trout's tail. Once I managed to bring him to hand, I simply opened the noose and off he went little the worse for wear.

The other story that's tied for weirdest also occurred on Ridley Creek, in the same pool now that I think of it. (I'm not sure if some powerful cosmic force is focused there or if I just spend an inordinate amount of time fishing in that location.) I was nymph fishing and on one drift I snagged the bottom. After several fruitless attempts to free the hook from the streambed, I decided to break off rather than wade out and disturb the water I was fishing. I tied on a new fly, and several casts later I hung up again. This time I was able to free my fly, but as it was coming in I could tell that something extra was at the end of the leader. Imagine my surprise and amazement to discover that I'd hooked the fly I'd just lost, bend to bend, thus recovering it.

We've all had bats darting around us as we fished a good hatch at dusk. But I actually caught one. I was fishing a Sulphur hatch one evening, now that I think of it, at the same place on Ridley as the last two events. (You know, this is starting to get *really* scary.) On one backcast I at first thought I'd snagged a tree branch, but when I turned to see where the trouble was I could see a bat flying at the end of my leader like an animated kite. In a moment the bat fluttered down to the ground. I managed to hand-over-hand the leader until he was close enough for me to very gently pin his wing to the ground with my boot. He was hooked in the tail membranes, so I reached down with my clamps and easily backed out the barbless hook. I lifted my foot off his wing and he hopped away into the shrubbery and I was back in business with the trout.

I didn't make too much of that at the time, assuming that the bat had simply flown into my backcast and gotten foul-hooked. I should have known that such a skilled predator would not be so clumsy. It couldn't have been more than a week later when I was watching a PBS documentary about wildlife photography and one of the segments was about the mechanics of how bats feed. Everyone knows about bats finding their prey by echolocation. But no one had found out how they actually *caught* the prey. Did they grab it directly with their mouth; gather it in with their wings, or what? Ultra high-speed photography revealed that bats scoop up their prey in flight *with their tail membranes*! So I did not foul-hook that bat, he intended to eat my fly. I *caught* him. I must say, however, that I'm *really* glad he didn't have time to put the fly into his mouth before the line came tight.

My final weird fishing tale, you'll be glad to know, did not occur on the Bridge Pool of Ridley Creek. It happened at the second bridge on Cedar Run in North Central Pennsylvania. My buddy Don Kaiser and I had gone up to fish the Sulphur spinner fall on Cedar that evening. As so often happens, the closer we got to darkness the faster and more furious the fishing became. Finally I could no longer see my fly on the water, although I could still hear slurping rises out in front of me. I already had my cast measured out, and used a favorite tactic for such situations. Lay the fly on the water and count: one-two-three and lift. It's amazing how often you can hook another few trout this way. Sure enough, on one cast I lifted and there was live weight at the end of my line. But it didn't feel right. It wasn't heavy enough to be a typical trout, and it wasn't acting like a fish at all. I retrieved my line until I could lift my fly from the water and see what I had. Dangling on the end of my leader was a frog, hanging upside-down by his left hind foot and making pitiful swimming motions with his front legs. I released this unusual catch and called it a night.

I'm sure that most of our DVWFFA members have strange fish tales of their own. If you'd like to share yours, send them to me and if I get enough responses I'll collect them into another article like this one. *Please,* reassure me that stuff like this happens to other people?

Winter 2008

End of a Season
By Rabbit Jensen

It was an invigoratingly cold morning in mid-October. Two friends, Lois and Nathalie, in my car, I drove down Benson Road under a canopy of gold, red, and bronze. Sun illuminated the foliage like stained glass and streamed down on the fallen leaves carpeting the road. It was my first trip to Young Woman's this year, and it felt right. For me, this is a stream of emotion as much as it is a stream of water. My senses are sharper when I fish here than anywhere else, and every little occurrence seems to have significance beyond the mundane.

Though I knew I wouldn't be wading nearly deep enough to need them, I hauled on the chest waders: one more layer between me and the cold air. The three of us shared our gloves, flies, and fishing tips, then split up. There's plenty of good water on this stretch, which divides and subdivides into a half-dozen channels, most holding trout. Small pools; holes gouged by tree roots, deadfalls, or rocks; hemlock overhanging runs; trout cover is everywhere.

It's rough country, challenging us as we clambered up and down out of these side channels, or former channels now dry, over deadfalls and treacherous rocks hidden by waist-high ferns or grass. But it's worth it on a golden day like this was, surrounded by warm colors in dozens of hues, with the frequent reward of a sudden side channel opening at our feet. The falling cadence of a hawk call punctuated the music of running water, or the tick-tick-tick of a leaf falling and striking its fellows on the way down, reminding us that fishing season was soon to end.

The Yellow Humpy settled perfectly against a slate bank, was swept a bare inch by the current, and was engulfed in a rise. I missed, my second miss of the day, but my smile was as happy as it was rueful. I'd found one more wild trout that had survived the drought of the past few years, and the treacherous draw-downs by the gas companies; one more to reproduce his threatened kind, and provide me with fishing next season. I silently blessed him, as he had just blessed me by rising to my fly.

Shortly I noticed the sunlight was muted, clouds building overhead. The rising humidity tickled my nose, and some atavistic instinct had me thinking more of returning to the car than fishing. I espied Lois, we agreed it was close enough to our rendezvous time, and hiked out together. Nathalie must have had the same idea, for we all met there, sharing our experiences as we shared our snacks: an excellent gruyere I carved with my penknife and handed around, bite by bite; a carefully-divided local apple; and Lois' home-made biscotti; a lunch embodying autumn, to my taste.

From there we drove onwards, to seek other streams, driving and walking through magnificent autumn scenery, sharing the camaraderie of women who fly fish. But, to me, as always, leaving Young Woman's meant leaving a sacred space, even after a fishless trip. Sometimes, it's the place, not the weight of the creel, that's important. In this case, the place, the people, and the time combined to weave the magic spell.

Twenty-four hours later, I sit in my living room marveling at six inches of snow on my lawn, at the incongruity of it clinging to leaves still yellowish-green on the trees in my front yard. Who could have predicted that yesterday's golden idyll would be the last trip of the season? Certainly the weatherman had not. But my tackle is still in the car, just in case the combination of an unseasonably warm day and cabin fever allow me to sample the magic just one more time.

Winter 2010

Just Google "Happiness"
By Mallory Briggs

I owe my interest in fly fishing to a man named Frank. I met Frank when I was working on a cattle ranch in Hyattville, Wyoming the summer I graduated from college. Working on a ranch had been a dream of mine since I was little, and this dream-come-true experience was sweetened by my introduction to fly fishing.

My introduction began when Frank, a retired Coca-Cola plant manager who lived in the next town over, walked into the ranch office one morning, uninvited, wearing a shirt with a fish on it, sunglasses, and a smile: "Who wants to learn how to fly fish?" A little nervous, but excited, I raised my hand.

Frank took me out about three times that summer, with a few casting practices before to warm up. We fished a creek on the ranch with a landscape of red cliffs jutting out on one side and pastures of wheat shimmering on the other. The occasional horse or cow would wander past, giving a sideways glance, but otherwise uninterested in the skill I was acquiring and all the fish I was catching. I guess the animals did not understand the excitement of what I was doing, or maybe they were just wondering what took me so long. When I left that summer, Frank told me to keep in touch, and to keep fishing.

I started law school at Villanova University that fall. I wanted to keep fishing, but the prospect of doing it on my own, buying all the equipment, and finding a place to go overwhelmed me. I let it slide for a while, unhappy with my lack of gumption and sad to disappoint Frank.

Sporadically, I tried to start. I was in New York City for an interview in the fall of my second year at law school and saw a fly shop on the corner. The interview went poorly, so in an attempt to console myself and do something right, I went in and came out with my first fly rod. A couple months later, I finally got up the courage to go out on my own. I cast my line in the beautiful river of Valley Creek in historical Valley Forge, hoping to impress the ghost of George Washington with my skill as an angler. Instead, I caught nothing, and the rain boots I was wearing as a cheap attempt at waders were soaked. But, I had started.

After this experience, I decided I needed some help; and by humbly entering fly fishing search terms in Google, I found the DVWFFA. I became a member and signed up for my first outing: "Summer Series I: Darby Creek" with Mary Kuss.

I met up with Mary and was immediately happy I had joined. This was a woman who was a veteran and loved it. Trying not to embarrass myself as we prepared, we put on our waders, set up our rods, and took a walk down a tree-lined, grassy lane along the water. Darby Creek is sandwiched between a sewer line and a busy highway, cars are whizzing by and spray paint marks are evident on the trail. Along with those same spray paint marks, however, we saw birds, frogs, and fireflies. We were fishing in a little piece of nature, a gem in the middle of the productive, developed world. And it was here, with helpful guidance from Mary, that I caught my first Pennsylvania fish, and not just one, but seven! This first trip showed me that not only will fly fishing be a part of my life, but the DVWFFA will provide me more than help, but also companionship and fun.

Autumn 2011

Fly Fishing Heaven
By Mary Gibney

In early 2009 I took a ride with Betsy Miraglia to the Allentown area to listen to a presentation by Don Baylor on fly fishing in western Colorado. It sounded so exciting I signed up immediately which is unusual since I'm not an impulsive person. When I said I would go, I had assumed we were going to get a group from DVWFFA, but we wound up joining six women from The Golden West Women Flyfishers, a women's fly fishing club in Northern California. The club was started by Fanny Krieger who was also the coordinator of the trip. We stayed in a cabin on a working cattle ranch that was a hundred yards from the Colorado River.

The first day of fishing Betsy and I were treated to a great float on the Colorado River with head guide, Barry Simmers. We caught a lot of big fish on Elk Hair Caddis or Stimulator dries with a small parachute Adams trailing. We didn't see anyone else on the water the whole day and I was in heaven. It was only my third float so I hid in the back of the boat and had a blast. I don't think we caught any fish that day under 16 inches. In the evening we got cleaned up and had dinner with the ranch owners in their home. The food was fresh and delicious every night and Mike and Anne Luark were gracious hosts. I had never gone away on an extended fishing trip and I couldn't get enough of it.

The second day I paired up with one of the California women and floated another section of the Colorado River. We were so spoiled with big fish after the first day I can remember we were both trying to get the tiddlers (14-inch and smaller fish) to unhook themselves. As I was floating and intently watching my fly which didn't budge, I felt my rod twitch. Confused by this I looked at my rod tip to find a hummingbird taking a rest there. How cool is that? As you all know, a lot of beautiful things happen while fly fishing.

The rest of the week Betsy and I were treated to three days of fishing with Don Baylor who kindly took us to fish the Yampa, Eagle and Colorado Rivers. We had a blast and I learned a lot.

In 2010 I took the trip again, but this time with DVWFFA members Betsy, Cheri Poole, Eleanor Peterson, Flora Soto and her husband, Ron. Unfortunately the rivers were off-color from heavy rains and pretty much unfishable the whole week. Thankfully there are plenty of other options out there. We fished mostly tailwaters and small streams and floated the Colorado once. Besides more great fishing, I also saw my first bear albeit safely from the car. On our drive up Colorado River Road to meet Barry the last morning, a cub ran in front of us and scampered up a nearly vertical mountain of red shale.

This July I made the trip alone and hired Barry for the week. He has been fly fishing for 50 years and guiding for 30 and after my experiences of the previous two years I had no reason to look further at destinations or guides. On top of that he has a great sense of humor, even though he did threaten to break my rod in half if I threw one more sidearm cast. After spending most of my fly fishing days on Valley Creek which is predominantly covered with tree canopy, the sidearm is my go-to cast so that was a difficult habit to attempt to break.

Since it was just the two of us I told Barry to fish with me. Again the rivers were mostly unfishable with the crazy runoff from the record snows so we fished tailwaters, some small mountain streams and one float on the Roaring Fork at the end of the week. Like the other years the fish were very accommodating. The first full day I caught the fat 5-pound brown in the picture on a secret tailwater nearby. It was my biggest trout landed ever, besides a steelhead. We also fished the Yampa, Frying Pan and Rock Creek, and caught rainbows, browns and brookies.

We went back a second day to the tailwater where I caught the nice brown. We started at the big pool and I had trouble locating my fly in the waves so I kept trying different flies. I sat down on the rocks to change flies and got summoned by "my guide" to net his fish. What is wrong with this picture? After this scenario happened three times I decided I needed to get out of there so *I* could actually fish. I carefully crossed the stream and headed to the other side of the pool. I proceeded to hook another brown as big as the first, but now I was on my own. I was fishing from rocks and couldn't get into the water or I'd have gone for a swim. After several long runs I got the brown halfway into my little Pennsylvania-size trout net three times before I broke off the fish. I was shaking and devastated and smashed my net onto the water with several expletives. Losing that fish kept me from falling asleep for at least two weeks. My arms were just not long enough to get under that fish. I have since invested in a bigger net with an extended handle and can't wait to get back to try again.

Autumn 2011

Are All Trout Created Equal?
By Rabbit Jensen

My first trout was from a fee-fishing place, obviously born and raised under human supervision. This didn't matter, it was a tug on the line; then a squirming, silvery creature, ineptly juggled as I struggled to remove the hook. Later that day, it was dinner, as I had a mentor who wisely introduced me early to the concept that fly-fishing is a predatory act at its root.

As time passed, though, I began to be less satisfied with this kind of catch. I had discovered there were trout-stocked streams, open to the public, where there would be competition for the trout. Where there were hatches to match (a new concept to me at the time), and fishing was more natural and sportsmanlike. This did not negate the pleasure of my first trout, but was the logical second step in my growth as an angler. I finally took my first public-waters trout from Ridley Creek on an Adams. This was a landmark in many other ways: I'd chosen the fly, and the approach, and I released that brown. I did not, as I would now, examine it to determine whether it was a freshly-stocked brown, a holdover, or one of Ridley's rare stream-bred browns. The important thing was the connection, as I looked into its eyes, admiring it, and became in one breath's time a life-long fly angler. The experience meant more than the origin of the fish.

For the novice, a trout is a trout is a trout. Many don't even know what *kind* of trout they are catching. It's in PFBC Approved Trout Waters and has spots, so it is a trout, not a shiner, fallfish, or any other denizen of the stream. But, gradually, as an angler gains experience, she begins to find differences in behavior, origin, and appearance that make some trout more desirable to catch than others.

When I was going through this stage, I didn't know what I was seeing at first. Trips to the Yellow Breeches yielded a few trout in the eleven-to-twelve inch range, hard fighters as might be expected by their size compared to the cookie-cutter 9-inch stockies I was used to catching. Were these holdovers or just the sparse salting of larger fish included in every stocking? In retrospect I can't tell. I also caught a few undersized fish, eight-inchers. Were a few runts mixed in with catchable-sized trout in stocking, or did I land stream-bred trout? Again, I was too ignorant to know the difference and just beginning to care. Finally, in an inaccessible spot on Ridley Creek, I caught a seven-inch brown with a few orange spots among the dark ones, a slender body and comparatively large head, and smooth-edged, oval pectoral fins. This was the prettiest brown I'd caught to date, and, incidentally, the first trout on a fly pattern I'd designed myself. I had landed one of Ridley's few wild trout, and knew from conversation how rare they were. This was a special fish because of its origins and rarity.

After that, I paid closer attention to the trout I caught. Although I fished only Approved Trout Waters, I rapidly began to notice superior fighting ability in holdover fish. They were also the ones that were in predictable places, feeding on insects. Remember, stocked trout are reared in raceways. This has more effects than the physical ones like tattered fins and faded coloring. It conditions their little trout minds to regular, artificial food, and holding in deep water with vertical sides. Freshly stocked trout instinctively seek the same conditions. That's why the 'honey hole' phenomenon. It's the closest these fish can come to the comforts of home, and never mind that they are in the hole fin-to-fin; they are used to that, too. The poor things wait in vain for their twice-daily pellets. Having no idea what else they can eat, they are often arbitrary and whimsical about what flies they will take.

A trout that survives this sink-or-swim introduction to a natural environment is rare, and extraordinarily lucky. It just happened to mouth a passing nymph and found out it was tasty. It somehow avoided sampling anything with a hook in it, somehow avoided mergansers, herons, and other natural predators, and found proper cover from these critters. In marginal waters like so many south-eastern Pennsylvania streams are, it made it through the warm, low, waters of summer. Any trout that makes it to fall is an intelligent and lucky fish, indeed, and a valuable one. I'll keep freshly-stocked trout, if I have a yen for a fish dinner, but I release hold-overs. They are proven survivors.

Once an angler reaches this stage, it becomes important to differentiate between types of trout and know their habits. Rainbow trout are my eating trout because almost all have been bred for the last century from steelhead root stock; their instinct is to 'follow their tails' downstream. Stock them today, and next week they will be as much as two miles downstream. They are bred for the skillet, and that's where I put them. Browns at least have the potential to hold over in marginal waters, and I always release them. Stocked brookies in most south-eastern Pennsylvania streams are more susceptible to high temperature water and usually don't make it through the summer. A stocked brookie is usually obvious, being comparatively large and possessing fins with tattered edges. I may release them in fall, to grow larger by spring, but in marginal waters these are sometimes also on my menu.

Four years after I caught that first trout, I took a trip to the Pennsylvania Wilds (long before they were called that) and discovered fishing streams with much less angling pressure than the ones I was accustomed to. Some of these were on the PFBC approved list, such as Kettle Creek, in which I caught a wild brown that was everything a wild trout should be: strong as a stocked trout half again his size, rising freely in a lie offering cover and access to deep water nearby, and close to a current bringing insects for consumption; when landed, he had bright orange and red spots sprinkled among the black ones, and all his fins were smooth-edged and golden.

It was not until years later that I began to seriously venture beyond Approved Trout Waters, and discovered the solitary joys of fishing for truly wild fish, beyond the stocking truck. Most of these are brook trout, our sole native Pennsylvania species. It gives me great satisfaction to know that they can trace their ancestry back millennia, without raceways or pellets. Why is this important? They are genetically selected to thrive in Pennsylvania streams. They will be found in cover close to feeding lanes, as trout are supposed to be, and feed on the predominant insect species at any given place and time. In short, they act like trout are supposed to act, as their wild ancestors did. In addition, they are exceptionally strong for their size and just plain lovely to look at. In Pennsylvania, they are almost never found in any but the wildest, least developed, prettiest areas, which is a bonus. A further plus is, few anglers fish for them, so I usually have these streams almost to myself.

So, in forty years of fly-fishing I've decided that all trout are *not* created equal. However, each must be respected and enjoyed for itself, in its own proper place. As an angler gains experience, one of the ways she continues to learn, and set and achieve new goals, is by seeking wilder trout, a more natural angling experience than fishing for stocked catchables. This progression of knowledge is one of the appealing things about fly-fishing: there is always more to learn, always more goals to achieve. Fresh delights await us all on the trout stream, without end.

Summer 2012

Bello Belize: Patience, Fun, and a Stroke of Good Luck Land the Permit
By Lisa Miller

When Betsy Miraglia and I started to talk about Belize, I thought it would be great fun to get away for a little bit and do a little fishing in a warm weather spot. Betsy had been last year so I knew I could learn a lot from her in addition to having a great time. I always enjoy striper fishing along the Chesapeake in the spring and I assumed all saltwater fishing would be similar. Boy, was I mistaken! Fishing for bonefish, permit, and tarpon are completely different fish from striper, and way more fun! Each requires strategy, patience, and good luck to land.

Our destination was the beautiful El Pescador resort on Ambergris Caye just off of the mainland near Belize City. We arrived on a beautiful spring day filled with expectations of catching fish; my hope was to catch a few bonefish. Everyone had told me to focus on bonefish as they are plentiful and because anything else was highly unlikely for a first-timer. Our guide Carlos took us to catch those bones on the first day. Our fishing location was a flats area that required sight fishing and patience. Betsy took the lead (I'm no dummy, I was learning by watching) and headed to the casting deck. After several casts, she landed a nice bonefish. It was my turn at the casting deck. Slowly, I headed up and realized for the first time that I was in a boat and there was movement. I hadn't experienced that motion when I practiced my double haul and quickly learned that it takes some getting used to when casting from a boat. My first cast was horrible and my assessment was confirmed pretty clearly when Carlos told me I was slapping the water with my line. Yes, I was coming down too hard (again), which only resulted in causing all the fish to *run*. A few minutes later I tried again but with no luck. I realized Betsy made it look way easier than it really is. After about a half hour, Carlos informed us that I'd basically done enough damage and had spooked the fish, so we were off to a different location. As we pulled off, I began to realize how unprepared I was for this trip, but tried to rationalize that we all have to start somewhere.

The second spot was much more productive for us. Carlos took us aside and covered the casting fundamentals again. With this and deeper water, I cast my rod, waited a moment, and stripped the line. I felt a tug so I 'strip set' the hook, and one more time for good luck. The bonefish ran like anything and then stopped. I gathered up the line and he ran again. I gathered up the line again and he decided to run one more time. This time, my thumb got in the way of the reel and I split my nail. I ignored the blood and worked the line in to land the bonefish. Then, between Betsy and me, it was a blitz to the finish. We figure we landed about fifteen fish. What a great day, that ended back at the resort with stories over beer, and dreams of the next day's big catch.

Day two turned out to be a bad casting day as Carlos pointed out repeatedly by telling us we were ten feet too short or too far to the right. Plus, I fell off the casting deck! It was a day of mistakes and disappointments. Nothing was on the end of the line.

Day three, we tried for permit before heading to tarpon territory. Permit are elusive. I was totally fascinated with the wave they make when traveling in schools. It's literally just a wave of water moving across the surface. We saw a couple waves and cast to them, but without luck as we were too short or not in the wave at all. So, we headed to tarpon territory, but first Carlos wanted to work with me to improve my double haul. On the casting deck, he shared tips for effective line shooting. On my last cast, I made him smile with my nice double haul that felt like it went 80 feet, but he assured me it was more like 40 feet; I can dream. For kicks, I stripped it in and voila, there was a tug at the end of the line so I set the hook (Mary Kuss says to *always* set the hook) in eager anticipation to see what was on the other end. *Whoosh*... this time, the fish took me clear through and well into my backing. I've never seen backing before and I was a bit confused as to how to bring all that line in. Slowly, I figured it out and after several minutes I landed my largest bonefish for the trip: 15 inches.

Day four and we were heading out again for permit. I was no longer sure why I was wasting my time on these permit because they're tough to see, tough to cast to, and tough to stay with when they are traveling at high speed. However, this time we were on a big school (a huge wave of permit) and Carlos was able to get close enough for our abilities. I watched Betsy work the casting deck and quickly hook a permit, but the permit threw the fly. After several more attempts, Betsy took a break and I headed to the deck to try my luck. I was amazed that I could see these fish and amazed at how Carlos had stayed with these fish and stayed so close to them. He was working so hard, so I decided to be patient, target my casts, and try my luck. It was magical; everything finally came together. I cast into the wave and got a hit. Next, I thought I heard Carlos tell me to 'let the line go.' While this advice seemed really wrong, I dropped the line out of my hands. I did this *three* times before actually losing the permit. (Carlos is still talking about how I, incredibly, put slack in the line.) Oh well, I gathered my focus and I cast again. This time, I was bound and determined not to get slack in the line. I got a hit, held on *too* tight and the fish broke the line. Yikes… I know that's not good. Third cast, I got the hit, set the hook, provided just enough tension, and brought the fish in. Yahoo, finally a fish... except it was a yellow jack. Apparently, there was no time for pictures because we were after the permit and this jack didn't count. Carlos quickly threw the jack back in, I cast the line, waited a bit, then a fish hit again, and this time it was a permit on the end of my line. Using proper tension and turning the fish away from the debris behind the boat, I brought the permit in; all 24 inches of permit. What a stroke of good luck!

Our last day was spent fishing for more bones in a deep area. It was like fishing in a barrel. I think Betsy and I landed about twelve each. Then, we headed to the channel for some possible sight fishing for bonefish. It was murky and I didn't see a thing, but I cast the line. After a couple casts, there was a tug, so I set it good and started working the fish that was running out the line. It didn't feel like a bone to me and I quickly saw that it was a permit. It was a nice-sized, but smaller permit. Who would have thought?

For me, this Belize trip was supposed to be a little bit of fishing and a couple days of snorkeling and Mayan ruin exploration. Before I went, I knew I would never be able to fish for seven days straight. Despite, or perhaps because of, the learning curve and all the mistakes with my fly fishing, I fished each day and had an amazing time. I couldn't wait to see what adventures were waiting for us on the flats. Betsy and I had a lot of laughs, met fascinating people, caught lots of fish, and had a lot of fun in the process. We are already planning our return trip!

Summer 2012

October Colors
By Rabbit Jensen

I always *think* I remember how brightly-colored and gorgeous the autumn leaves are, but every October the reality makes me realize my memory is only a pale copy. I drove along a familiar dirt road, the mellow sounds of Pink Floyd's *Wish You Were Here* the soundtrack to autumn's foliage show. The leaves were at peak color, and it was stunning. Every year I say daily, "It can't get any prettier than this," and every day it does, until the storm that usually strips the leaves away. In the North Woods, autumn ends with a blast, not a quiet, gradual fall; and it happens in the middle of October, which had just arrived. I was thinking that this could very well be my last trout trip of the year, so I was deep in that most poignant of pleasures, appreciating the "now."

In keeping with the natural beauty of my surroundings, I uncased my beloved Phillipson split-bamboo; affixing the Hardy Perfect reel with, as always, warm thoughts for the DVWFFA members who gave it to me. Walking in, I heard a kingfisher chirr near the island upstream of the bridge pool, then it flew up to perch a moment and show off for me. Asters and chamomile were blooming, and the crabapple trees at Creekview Camp were fruit-laden. Across the creek, the hillside blazed with color.

I went directly to last spring's new deadfall. It had changed already. It had shifted so that a branch prevented casting right up into the sweet spot, but the deep hole downstream and the secondary flow this side of the supporting log still had plenty of fish. The first one that hit my chartreuse-bodied Royal Wulff did so at the very moment a butterfly landed on my shoulder, distracting me. I think they were conspiring against me. A few minutes later I hooked and landed a parr-marked 6-inch male brookie. Several casts later, as I worked my way upstream along this cut, I had a 'long distance release,' a slightly larger brook trout. In that secondary current I missed an aggressive fellow that came charging up from the bottom to hit my fly, *twice*. I rested him a few minutes while probing the main current, then tried another float over him and hooked him this time. This was a respectable male brookie in the 8 or 9 inch range, highly colored and ready for fun. Like my memory falls short for the leaves this time of year, I always forget the true, vital beauty of wild brook trout colored up for spawning. They take those autumn colors and enhance them, add luster and depth, bestowing them on a strong, virile, living being. They are lovely any time of year, but in October they are sheer perfection. The hook was firmly buried in the corner-of-the-mouth cartilage; to reduce handling stress, I snipped the tippet after a few tries failed to extract it. The muscular male, who had so quietly endured handling, shot agilely from my hands when freed, proving his ability to survive.

I replaced this fly with a more traditional Royal Wulff, landing one more brookie before moving upstream. The diagonal log two-thirds up this long pool was shifted parallel to the bank last spring, but the hole it dug over the years is still there, a secret known only to those who have fished here often in the past. I landed two trout here, the second of 7 or 8 inches, both males in spawning colors.

I decided to hike downstream to the blue trailer, which is apparently called 'Cut Loose Camp,' although I call it Jake's Hole after the old friend that told me about it. There is an intriguing arrangement of boulders along this stretch including a particularly deep plunge pool and downstream trough. I haven't had any luck here in the past, and was fishing along grumbling, "I know there're fish in here! There's *got* to be a fish in here!" As I lifted the rod for another cast, the fly refused to come out of the water. I grabbed the line to tug gently and free the fly from whatever obstacle it had penetrated, and it was a fish! I hand-lined it in, a feisty male brookie in the 7-inch category.

Some number of casts later I missed another charge-up-from-the-bottom hit. Once again I rested the fish, then tried a few more floats over the same spot. The fourth cast, déjà vu, only this time I hooked him, a dogged fighter. I was astonished to land my first brown trout from this stretch since 2008, a nine-inch wild fish with sparse, large black spots and a few orange ones. A few minutes later, I hooked a larger fish, which appeared to be another brown, another LDR.

I was tired, and deerflies were chomping my unprotected hands. I went back up to Creekview Camp, where I had a single hit. I changed flies twice, with no improvement. By now my back and feet were really painful, and the deerflies had not lost interest in me, either. Trudging out, I was undecided whether I'd have the stamina to fish K-Kamp Run all the way up to the bridge pool. I sat on the bench at K-Kamp studying the water, soaking in the autumn colors, and listening to a grouse drumming. Every few minutes, I'd hear the almost-subliminal, increasing-tempo beats. I used to believe they only drummed in spring, but learned otherwise after moving up here. Gradually October's beauty, that surprisingly harmonious blend of gaudiness and serenity, seeped back into my soul. Tiredness, pain, even those pesky deerflies, diminished and faded into the background.

Water levels were high and fast, by autumn standards. I decided the run in front of me should fish well under those conditions, so I worked my way down the neck-breaker steps and waded well out. This featureless-looking run actually hides a number of deep pockets and cuts, and I positioned myself to cover several of the best. My first fish took the first cast. I'd lost track of the fly in the glare and struck just because the fish did one of those Orvis-logo jumps. It turned out it had indeed taken my fly, a fine brookie of 7 or 8 inches. Another strike at a breaching trout, and I landed a typical six-incher. Of course, I missed a couple hits this way as well.

There's a secret deep pocket on the right, and I was perfectly placed to cover it. A confident rise, a well-timed strike, and I knew right away that this was the biggest fish of the day. "This is my quitting fish," I said aloud, with great satisfaction, as the struggling trout put a lovely bend in my cane rod. There was no rushing this fellow, who turned out to be 11 inches of wide-shouldered, gorgeous, and powerful male brook trout. And I told him so, as I released him.

I waded out and trudged back to the car, exhausted, achy, and totally happy. It was indeed to be my last fishing trip of a memorable year, a fitting high note to end on. The impossible beauty and strength of those wild trout, amidst the glories of an October day, would live in my memories through the long, cold months indoors. Only to be surpassed next autumn, when I once again discover: I always *think* I remember how brightly-colored and gorgeous the autumn leaves are, but every October the reality makes me realize my memory is only a pale copy...

Autumn 2012

Observations
By Joan Hackmann-Gaul

Whenever I come upon a fly fisher with a beautiful cast, I stop and watch. I watch the curve of the line, the action of the rod, the arm of the fly fisher and the presentation onto the water. Voila! To me it is a dance; a ballet. But, there is a lot more that goes into this dance. There is the movement of the water, the surroundings of the flora and fauna, the smell of the stream, the tranquility, especially when it is during an evening rise; and being alone, alone to focus on just one thing: fishing.

Tom Boyd recently wrote an article for *The Denver Post* entitled *Lady and the Trout*. Tom interviewed Erica Stock of Trout Unlimited. "Fly-fishing is very restorative. It's not a race. It's not a competition. It's meant to relax you… it has a meditative quality… you have to remember that you will never achieve perfection, so you have to go into a kind of Zen Buddhist mind-set."

There was a time when I thought the last one into the stream was a rotten egg. At the end of the day, the last one into the stream is most likely the better fly fisher. Over time, I have learned to take my time and review what flies or insects may work. I look over the stream for pools, rocks, tree limbs and bushes along the bank. Then I will ease myself into the water and become comfortable with the stream; making it all come together with the grip of the rod, the cast, the flow of the line, the dance.

As time goes by I will become a better dancer. I have learned patience, how to center-down, that time is not important, and knots are.

Winter 2014

Twilight
By Rabbit Jensen

In my twilight saga, there are no glittery vampires or neurotic, selfish teenage girls. In my world, summer twilight is a wholesome, nurturing time, uplifting and magical. This is true however I choose to spend that all-too-brief time, but especially true when fishing.

First comes the anticipation. The afternoon sunlight washes over me like warmed honey; it was sweet earlier but by this time of the day it's cloying. The trout rise sporadically, refusing my fly more often than they take it. If I've been fishing long, this is the time when I become tired, and wade ashore to munch a granola bar and swig some water. I squint at the lowering sun, peer at the water seeking signs of an imminent hatch, examine my terminal tackle, and pore over my fly boxes. Much of the time I know what's due to hatch, and this is the breathing space I use to hook a couple of flies matching the predicted hatch in the 'fly trap' clipped to my vest, ready to grab quickly when (and if) the event begins. Sometimes I'll actually tie one on, but until a hatch actually manifests itself, I normally stick with the fly I've been using, even if I've had lackluster response to it.

As predictable as hatches are in general, when a fly angler gets down to a specific stretch of a certain stream on a given evening, 'the organism does what it damn well pleases.' We can only take what Nature gives us. The uncertainty is a big part of the allure: Will it happen at all? Will the fish do their part? Will this evening be uneventful, slow, or one of those miracle nights that stay in memory forever? And, always, for me, there's the uncertainty of whether I have the right fly, the right skills, to take advantage of that miracle. At this stage of the process, I'm focused on the goal, but I remind myself that being out there is *always* worthwhile, hatch or no, fish or no.

Then it happens. There is a sudden lull in the wind, literally a pause for breath, and the fish sense it, too. The little feeding they have been doing ceases. The quality of the light has changed, too subtly to describe, but noticeably. A swallow swoops low across the stream. Then another, and another. Finally I spot what the swallows have already seen:

Two mayflies fly above me, silhouetted against the pale blue sky, locked together in conjugal bliss, and more linked pairs soar around them. I smile, sending them a blessing that they might escape the hungry swallows and lay tens of thousands of eggs. Then, when their life's purpose is done, feed a hungry trout!

Right on cue, a ring disturbs the water of the pool below me. My fatigue vanishes, I am energized. This is not the time for haste, though. I walk down to the tail of the pool, wade in step by slow, quiet step. More fish are rising, and I watch and wonder: Are they on the spinners? The rise forms don't tell me this time, but I tie one on anyway.

With the first false cast, the magic happens. I vanish. More accurately, I become absorbed in and a part of the natural world, and any connection I have to the complex, artificial world of human endeavor vanishes. It doesn't matter whether I catch fish. It doesn't matter how many flies I lose in trees, or even if I fall in and get soaked. What matters is the rapidly-changing texture of the light as the sun sets, the mayflies in their ecstatic dance of life and death and renewal, the fish sounding the final grace note for them. On some level I'm aware that the dying spinners keep the trout alive, trout that will spawn and renew the life of their kind in a few short months. And it is so for other predators; as light fades, the swooping swallows are joined by bats, both with similar roles to play, a part of the same cycle of life-death-life as the mayflies, the trout… and me. Not to mention the day, which is rapidly nearing its own end. There is no sadness or grief here, for the sun will rise again tomorrow. A year from now, the eggs being laid by these mayflies will have become mayflies themselves, and dance the same dance. And a new generation of trout, parr-marked and barely as long as my finger, will get their first taste of them.

In the mountains, twilight ends swiftly. There's a short time between sunset and darkness that feels almost surreal, the air having a glow that has little to do with light. Perhaps it's the departing soul of day illuminating the world with a final blessing. I do know that I savor it, even while continuing to cast. In moments, it's gone.

Trout continue to feed, as the mating swarm is only beginning to diminish. I can no longer see my fly, and cast by feel, strike by guess, listening for rises in the dark. Usually my fishing ends with a lost fly or Gordian tangle. I find myself suddenly back in the human world, as I wonder why the heck I'm standing in the middle of a stream in the dark, with unseen slick rocks underfoot to negotiate, then a thorn-bordered trail between me and my car. I grip my wading staff with white knuckles as I slowly creep towards the bank, teetering and occasionally skidding, terrified of wading in the dark. The feeble light of a penlight leads me back to the metal-and-plastic security of that bastion of civilization, the car.

Yet, experiencing twilight has changed me. Cycles within cycles, death and renewal... these are more than words describing a sterile philosophy to me now. I've been immersed in them, become one with their lesson. When my own twilight comes, I will have no doubt that the sun will rise again.

Summer 2013

Vickie Bergeman takes a trophy wild brook
trout at twilight on Kettle Creek.

Early Season Memories
By Mary S. Kuss

There have been many constants in my fly fishing life. Cabin fever is one of them. Every winter I experience the same intense, restless longing for the season to get underway. The Holidays offer some welcome distraction. Then suddenly the hubbub is over, the decorations have been taken down, and the seemingly endless months of January and February stretch before me. Ice, snow, and cold winds drag on and on.

I take some small consolation in searching for signs that spring will eventually come. This is silly, really, because many of the changes in the natural world that augur the coming spring are apparent shortly after the time of the December solstice. The entire winter still lies ahead. These little signs are very subtle, and you would never notice if you were not watching for them. But watch I do, and each one I detect cheers me just a bit.

I tie flies, tinker with my fishing gear, browse my angling library and watch videos. There are fly fishing shows, club meetings, and other social activities with fellow anglers. I may even venture out streamside for a couple of hours on an unseasonably warm afternoon. But all of this seems rather unsatisfactory, like a tantalizing sip of water to someone dying of thirst.

If I do go fishing in winter, the stream usually shows few signs of life. The water looks cold and barren, even if there are a few midges in the air. The fish are still there, however, laid up in the deep holes that form their hibernacula—the places where they spend the winter. The right presentation, the right fly, in the right place and time, can bring a trout or fallfish or two. It doesn't scratch the itch nearly enough.

Sometimes midges hatch in sufficient quantity to bring some fish to the surface to sip the drifting pupae. The water is low and crystal clear, the fish fussy and spooky. Cold fingers and toes make concentration difficult, and tying a tiny fly to a gossamer tippet with numbed fingers is a real challenge. Fish rise to the midges with a slow but steady pace. Their feeding lacks the urgency it will have when the weather is warmer. Their metabolism is slow now, and they really don't need to eat much. The fly has to be right, and the presentation must be accurate, delicate, and synchronized with their feeding rhythm.

Spring approaches, inevitably. Ice may still line the stream's edge, yet buds are swelling, and the Early Black Stoneflies appear. This is the first sizeable insect of the year, and they are greeted warmly by both fish and angler. One late winter day I found a large trout rising to stoneflies in the Bridge Pool of the Ridley Creek fly stretch. The fish held along the big rock outcrop along the left side of the pool, intercepting stoneflies that skittered across the surface of the water toward the shelter of the rock. I had tied up a few of my favorite stonefly imitations, with a dark grey dubbed body, a turn or two of dun hackle, and a roll of grey nylon stocking material as a wing. I caught the trout, a beautiful hold-over brown of about 16 inches. He was a chunky fish, well-fed and well-formed. His fins were full and golden, his body a symphony of color—a creamy belly, yellow ochre flanks shading to raw umber, speckled with blackish and crimson spots. Two weeks later, same location, same hatch, same fly pattern, and what must have been the same fish. I released him with gratitude for the opportunity he gave me—twice! I still have both flies.

The classic early season parade of hatches comes next, if you are able to be on a stream where they occur. Ridley Creek used to have many of them, but the Dark Hendricksons and Quill Gordons I used to see there are no longer present. There has simply been too much development in the watershed. Too much silt, too much heavy run-off scouring the streambed. The sensitive insect species are gone. Yet with a bit of travel I can still find them.

One year I was in Potter County in April for the Women's Fly Fishing Clinic at Kettle Creek Lodge. The weather had been cold and wet, but one afternoon on Young Woman's Creek we met an excellent hatch of Blue Quills. Fish were rising, and the emerger pattern I had tied up in anticipation of the hatch worked perfectly. A good percentage of the risers we covered took the fly confidently.

Then there was an early-May DVWFFA event at the Ressica Falls Scout Reservation, in the Poconos, on the Big Bushkill Creek. The weather was cool and damp, and the Quill Gordons were hatching. The big duns were having a hard time getting off the water. They were being swept over the falls, and the drowned flies were carried into a large river-right back eddy. We had a field day, pulling trout after trout from the eddy with size 10 Quill Gordon wet flies.

Bugs don't always mean fish, though. A trip to the Upper Delaware with Ann McIntosh during one early-May gave us a day on the river when the surface of the water was peppered with Quill Gordons, Hendricksons, and Grannom caddis. Yet we found almost no trout feeding regularly. There was an occasional, sporadic rise, but no "targets"—fish holding station and rising in a regular rhythm. We tried searching the water with dry flies, nymphs, emergers, streamers. No dice.

We drifted along, sure that things had to start happening soon. Then I spotted a rise off a grassy point. I called it and our guide got us anchored up quickly. The fish popped again, and yet again. "Try him," I said to Ann.

"No, you saw him first, you try him," she replied.

I had one of the guide's Grannom imitations on my leader. "Should I show him the Grannom?" I asked.

"Yes," the guide replied shortly.

It took a few attempts before I got the cast right, and I knew it when I did. The fly drifted down toward the fish's station. I had only a few precious seconds of drift before drag would set in. "Now would be a good time," I said aloud.

It was as if the fish had heard me. I saw him turn toward me and loom up under the fly, and everything snapped into slow motion. I saw his white mouth open, saw him inhale the fly, saw him turn down. I felt as though I had all the time in the world. I brought the line tight, and the fight was on. After a spirited battle, the guide slipped the net under a fine 17-inch brown. It was the only trout we put in the boat all day long.

Spring marches on, then summer, and during the height of the season good fishing days can come with such regularity that they all run together. It takes something really special to stand out among such riches. By fall one is sated with good fishing. But the long cold winter always sharpens the appetite anew. Early season memories are the sweetest and the strongest.

Spring 2013

A Blind Date with Mr. Brown
By Rabbit Jensen

It had been three years since Mary Kuss's last trip to Potter County. Three years of watching her mother decline and finally pass away, then handling her grief and the estate, a long unhappy process. When she won the two-nights free stay at Kettle Creek Lodge in the DVWFFA Holiday Gathering raffle, she was well ready to return to her normal pursuits and her former haunts. E-mails flew between her, Laura Benna, and me, deciding just when was the best time to be here. We settled on the second week of June, the very end of my annual Spring Open House for Club members.

It was then I began formulating The Plan. For awhile I've had a long-distance relationship with a large wild brown trout in a certain small but deep pool on Kettle Creek. Some of you may remember Mr. Brown, as I wrote about him last fall, vowing I'd be prepared for another 'date' with this fabulous free-riser this year. But, the only thing I love more than catching a big wild trout is seeing a good friend catch one of 'my' pet fish. Wouldn't it be great if I could set up Mary for a date with Mr. Brown? My career as a Yenta was born!

After three years of mild, dry winters, winter 2013 went back to normal and then some, with record numbers of days below zero locking snow into ice. Copious spring rains plus persistent snow pack sent streams into roaring spate levels that went on and on. Would the streams be fishable even by the end of May? Or would Mary's long-planned and much-needed trip wash out? I was relieved when the rains tapered off and the water levels began to fall a scant two weeks before her arrival. The weather forecast for that week was not ideal, but we went ahead as planned.

After such a winter and spring, hatches were disrupted, watercourses altered, and it's possible the shallowest areas of streams experienced 'anchor ice.' Our first few days of fishing were lackluster, although scenery, wildlife-watching, and comradeship made up for the scarcity of caught fish. A favorite spot that had produced some nice big wild brookies for me ten days before yielded Mary a dozen or so smallish trout, but otherwise we fished hard for little reward. The stretches that she had been dreaming about for three years were a great disappointment. However, I still had The Plan. I still had my ace in the hole: my favorite section of upper Kettle Creek and Mr. Brown. By her last day, I had talked her into fishing there, although I was keeping The Plan a surprise.

As we stood on the rickety bridge there, examining spider webs for evidence of current hatches, I revealed The Plan to her. She was skeptical, I could tell. She knew about Mr. Brown, knew he was a pet of mine whom I'd never actually caught, and she did not want to poach on 'my' designated fish. I believe she also doubted my suggestion she try a dry fly, as she tactfully suggested we hike down and see what was happening before she chose a fly to use. I smothered my smile, hid my excitement. This was it: She was set up for the blind date I'd been planning for so long!

We arrived at what I call Jake's Place, the pool in front of the blue trailer. I pointed out the overhanging branch festooned with rusting streamers, the downstream run with its population of Mr. Brown's progeny, the upstream chute where a precisely-placed dry fly would float right over his home. I could tell that Mary finally comprehended the seriousness of the occasion. She refused to try for the youngsters downstream, opting to go right for the big fellow.

The discarded shucks of Isonichia we'd been seeing on rocks, the Slate Drakes caught in the spider webs, and my advice prompted her to choose her Parachute Slate Drake, a big, luscious-looking mouthful of dry fly. She stooped low, creeping slowly into position, and laid out a perfect cast. It floated through the pool unmolested. Another, lightly placed in just the right spot, went down untouched. But, third cast lucky! The big dry vanished in a confident rise.

"Is it?... is it?... it is! It's Mr. Brown!" On the bank, I was beside myself. One after another, I took photos that would tragically never come out due to my unfamiliarity with Mary's camera. Her crouching to cast; the first U-shaped bow in the rod as Mr. Brown dove deep; a splashing boil almost a yard across as he came to the surface; more trembling, straining bowed rod shots; then, finally, her bending down, the trout half-out of the water, as she prepared to lift him for a grip-and-grin shot before release.

With a quick twist, he came loose, swimming away back to his watery home, tired, wiser, but still free.

"He was in my hand. I count that as caught," Mary said, looking at the pool.

"All we missed was the picture," I agreed. "If I'd had a net, we would have gotten it. But, there's less stress on Mr. Brown this way. May he live many healthy years and spawn many like himself."

"Amen," Mary said, with nothing less than reverence. Then, she gave me a sidelong glance. "You set me up. You said he was at least fourteen inches, and he was well over that and heavy, too. Right where you said, and he took a dry fly cast right where you told me to put it."

"I did set you up," I confessed. "But it was your skill that caught him. I just had the pleasure of witnessing it." I waved the camera, unknowing that my photographic efforts had been in vain. "That was The Plan all along: a blind date with Mr. Brown."

Mary then said many more complimentary things about my guiding, but I well know whose fishing expertise caught Mr. Brown. I'd had that figured into The Plan.

Autumn 2014

The Beauty of the Experience
By Rabbit Jensen

When I look around at my fly-fishing friends, one thing that strikes me is that they are all creative people. They express this in widely different ways. There are woodcarvers, painters, potters, writers, a paper-maker, knitters, poets, gardeners, musicians, and people who just focus on making their home an esthetically pleasing place. It's based on an appreciation of beauty, as well as an inner drive to get hands-on involved with it. Some folks might say this is because I fish almost exclusively with other women, but my favorites among the male anglers I've known fit this profile, too. It just takes a little more digging to reveal their inner esthete sometimes.

The artistic personality is marked by an ability to focus, intently and to the exclusion of mundane distractions. At the same time, being able to *see*, in detail and to a level that other people usually miss, is what divides creative art from making copies. Both these traits make for a successful fly fisher. But beyond all analysis, beyond mechanical aptitude or skill, there lies something more: an attitude, an emotion. It's what moves us, what drives us, the 'why' of creativity… or fly fishing.

Why fly fishing as opposed to any other way of extracting fish from water? Or, for that matter, instead of golf, motorcycle riding, or watching football? For many of us, it's the sheer beauty of the experience we treasure. The exquisite natural surroundings, the graceful curving movements of casting, the delicate loveliness of the insects and the flies we use to imitate them; the eternal baroque improvisation of running water and the gentle musical swish of fly line; the romance of wooing the fish, the passion of the fight, then victory for both angler and fish, as we fall in love with the handful of shimmering life. Then, as the poster of my youth said, if you love something, let it go…

Fish are indeed beautiful. I love the power and fury of a leaping bass, that somehow reminds me of the male lead of a Russian ballet troupe I saw as a child, or Michael Flately at his peak; suspended impossibly in the air, all muscle and passion. I adore the brilliant colors of sunfish, 60's-psychedelic colors right out of a Peter Max painting, and their

I-can-do-anything attitudes. I often think that if sunnies were as big as they imagine they are, they'd be scary. I have great respect and affection for subtly beautiful wild brown trout, transplanted from Europe but adapted to American streams, wily enough that one can be born in a stream, live and grow old there without ever tasting the iron of a hook.

None of these are hatchery fish. They are born into and adapted to their environment, which is one of the intangible factors that make them lovely to my mind. Best of all in that respect is our native brook trout, evolved for eons to fit perfectly in its ecological niche, and with colors and presence that can never really be captured in pictures. I can't explain to most people why I eschew stocked streams where I might catch what we used to call 'wall-hanger' trout. I can't explain to some other anglers why I avoid dredging with weighted terminal tackle tipped with oh-so-effective nymphs and streamers. I certainly can't explain to *anyone* brush-busting my way to a remote creek barely ankle-deep to catch a trout no longer than my hand from a pool the size of a kitchen sink. Art? Or madness? Is there a difference?

All I know is that, for me, my motivation for fishing is the beauty of the experience. Since beauty is a subjective thing, my definition includes gorgeous wild fish, solitude, natural surroundings, light tackle and lighter flies, careful stalking, and delicate presentation, followed, with luck, by a rise. That may not be true in every detail for every angler I know, for each of them defines beauty in their own way; but I'd be willing to bet that the root motivation, the 'why I fly fish,' of all my fly angling friends is the same: the beauty of the experience.

Spring 2015

About the Editor

Rabbit Jensen started fly-tying as an art form in 1971 and began fishing with her creations in 1972. In 1999 she began guiding and instructing in Potter County, Pennsylvania, where she now resides. She is a familiar sight fly-tying at local shows, and was one of the featured fly tiers at the Pennsylvania Fly Fishing Museum grand opening. She is a Life Member of Trout Unlimited; former President of the Delaware Valley Women's Fly Fishing Association, and is its current newsletter editor. She's been writing about her fly-fishing experiences for nearly twenty years.

Rabbit began writing at the age of nine and the following year joined the staff of the school newspaper. She continued in journalism throughout her school years, including several years editing her high school's literary magazine and contributing a regular feature in her college newspaper. Once in the work world, her writings frequently appeared in the company magazine, and she was editor of the quarterly for her union local of nearly 2,000 members. Currently she edits two other small newsletters, writes for magazines, ghost-writes websites and publicity material, and keeps up a blog.

She retired from her full-time job in 2009 and moved to the Pennsylvania Wilds, where she lives surrounded by public forests and wild trout streams. When not fly-fishing she enjoys geocaching, photography, birding, hunting, and the indoor pursuits of reading, do-it-yourself projects, crafts, and spending time with her six cats.

Printed in the United States
By Bookmasters